GOOD TO THE LAST DROP

Living in Mortality's Shadow

Garry Cooper

SPUYTEN DUYVIL
New York City

The following chapters, in altered form, appeared in these magazines:

An Ambush of Mercy in *Psychotherapy Networker* (July/August 1996); Giving Up the Reins in *Psychotherapy Networker*; The Empty Nest in *Bloodroot* (v3, 2010); Hope at the Edge in *Triquarterly* (winter 2014) and in *Eulogy for Nigger and Other Essays*, Notting Hill Editions (2015); The Home Field in *Another Chicago Magazine* (June, 2019); Pandemic Report in *Another Chicago Magazine* (April, 2020); Cherry Blossoms, in *Fatal Flaw* (July, 2020)

It is rare to find essays that are wise, deep, and entertaining. Garry Cooper delivers these attributes and more in his meditations and narratives on the nature of love, loss, self-repair, mortality, and what we owe to one another. His essays are relatable but not simple. Unusually, he is also able to bring to life his delight in cities as well as in the indifferent silence of nature. By the end of the book, you will feel that you know him well, and know yourself better.

S.L. Wisenberg
author of *The Adventures of Cancer Bitch*

Most memoirs are simply that: an individual's recollection of portions of their lives that they hope are interesting enough to share with others. But when an experienced psychotherapist, backpacker, and hitchhiker writes his memoir, he offers more than his own experiences and dramas. From the opening scene of a harrowing lost-in-the-wilderness-and-making-stupid-mistakes tale to a cancer diagnosis to simply facing the knowledge that you have fewer years ahead of you than behind, themes of mortality echo throughout *Good to the Last Drop*. Recognizing that "We have a unique challenge: figuring out how to live through our final days," Cooper spins his tales and reflections with humor and insights gained over decades of fatherhood, therapy and, yes, his fair share of mistakes, seeking experiences in nature, hitchhiking, and sensory deprivation tanks. He shows some of the techniques he's used to recover (often slowly) from break-ups and grief ("Aches and pains reminded me in a good way that I was alive—signs of repair going on, not the harbingers of worse things to come. I remembered when optimism was a gateway to the future, not a survival strategy for getting through the present.") He asks, If you die tomorrow more than once. As we're all facing death through climate change, aging, and accidents he counsels, "Ultimately the most important thing is how we will go through our end times." Highly recommended for anyone seeking to approach their own times with grace, good humor, and deliberation.

Anara Guard,
author of *Like a Complete Unknown* and *Kansas, Reimagined*

For Alexandra Naomi Cooper
She makes the world a better place

*Nel mezzo del cammin di nostra vita mi ritroval per una
selva oscura, che la diritta via era smarrita. Ah! quanto a dir
qual era e cosa dura esta selva selvaggia e aspra e forte che nel
pensier rinnova la paura! Tanto e amara, che poco e più morte;
ma per trattar del ben chi vi trovai, dirò dell'altre cose ch'i v'ho
scorte.*

In the middle of the journey of life, I found myself in
a shadowed forest, where the path which does not stray
was lost. It is a hard thing to speak of, how savage, harsh
and impenetrable that forest was: even thinking of it now
renews my fear. It is scarcely less bitter than death: but if I
wish to tell of the good that I found there, I must also tell of
the other things I saw.

Dante's *Inferno* Canto One

PART FIVE: WALKING INTO CLIMATE CHANGE

Living Well While the Hourglass Trickles   285

PART SIX: THE LAST DROP

Sisyphus and his Fate   345

EPILOGUE

GOOD TO THE LAST DROP

LIVING IN MORTALITY'S SHADOW

INTRODUCTION:
THE BARREL

My father used to tell me that I was always falling into a barrel of shit and coming out smelling like a rose. I think he meant it as a compliment. Looking back on my life, I'm not convinced it was an accurate description of how I've lived, but it's an interesting organizing principle. This cycle of shit and roses (the second part of the cycle usually took a longer time to happen than the first) has happened with my loves, jobs and, about five years after my father's death, a solitary backpacking trip in New Mexico's Pecos Wilderness when I literally found myself at the brink of death.

I was 48 years old and hopelessly lost in the Pecos, starving, wet, and suffering from exposure so badly that I'd been hallucinating. It was late afternoon, and it came time to decide whether to struggle through another miserable chilly night or allow myself to slip into a coma. The decision was all mine, that simple, and a coma seemed preferable, like snuggling into a goose down comforter. But then I surprised myself and decided to try to survive at least a little longer. At the moment, my reasoning seemed absolutely clear: I suddenly felt I didn't have the right to leave my five and a half year old daughter back home in Chicago with such an abrupt loss, such a permanent hole in her life. But over the years I came to realize that the reasons for my decision had been considerably more complex than that.

I remember watching an intelligent, highly rational person buying a lottery ticket, and before he chose his numbers, he closed his eyes and relaxed, believing he was opening himself to his intuitive connection with whatever. For some people it's comforting to believe that conscious, rational decision-making steers their ship. Others believe in a god, fate or karma. Others cede the throne to the unconscious. Except for the most seriously depressed, we all, with varying levels of success, seek the comfort or the confirmation of our beliefs and hopes.

Now that our entire species has fallen into a barrel of shit, we're up against three questions:

Other than denial or hope, what keeps us from giving up?

In the next few decades, will it still be possible to live well?

And if so, how?

My own reason for deciding why I decided to go on living, while it seemed perfectly clear at the time, hasn't calcified into any one thing—that's the stuff of motivational speakers, emojis, self-help books and syrupy greeting cards. At various times, I'm still curious, dumbfounded, excited, bummed out, hopeful, and apprehensive about where my daughter's and my own life are heading. I usually manage, though sometimes with difficulty, to keep discovering why I want to be here and what, if anything, I should do with that. In his final days Timothy Leary, the LSD Pied Piper, knew he was dying, and he said that that moment between when his heart would stop beating and his brain would shut down were unexplored, and he was looking forward to finding out more about it.

In my psychotherapy practice, I try to remind myself that I'm not wise enough to know the right path or the deepest truth for any client. Each person's path and truth isn't necessarily fixed, and we discover their story together. In these times of aging demographics, a world-wide declining birth rate, diminishing resources and climate change, we're all approaching the fulcrum of life and death, and people are facing it with bucket lists and adventures, denial, despair, dog-eat-dog determination, sorrow, anxiety, greed, depression, hedonism, love, addiction, platitudes or bromides. It's good to have choices, right?

Good to the Last Drop invites you to walk along with me and to think more deeply about your own journey. It provides some hints to help you think about what might work better for *you* while you, and all of us, are living in the growing shadow of mortality. *The Last Drop* offers salvation, as long as we understand that salvation doesn't mean eternity.

PART ONE:
CONTEMPLATIVE TEMPLATES

Tipping Points and Ballasts

We all experience tipping points in our lives. When we lose our balance, we may seek ballasts that keep us from tipping over completely and help us steady our course. Children, however much they can unmoor us, are a common ballast. On its most basic level, the drive to have children is a biological imperative for perpetuating our species. Birds do it, bees do it, even educated fleas do it, along with hippopotamuses, sperm whales, rutting deer and, in their own way, paramecium. But human beings, possibly unique among all living things in knowing about our mortality, decide to have children for more complex reasons.

Love, as ubiquitous as children, is another ballast. (Part Three has more to say about that).

Think of tipping points as rehearsals for that final tipping point we'll all encounter. The French call orgasms la petite mort; we create life with our little deaths. So we try to extend our lease on life in perpetuity. We have children, and we hang portraits of ourselves, our ancestors and our history on walls, affix them in photograph albums or, less resonantly and permanently, store them on hard *drives or in the Cloud. (The worst of us try to postpone and extend mortality by accumulating more and more money or power).*

We all want something to hold on to, and to be remembered by. We hope, sometimes eagerly and sometimes desperately, that the things we've done, and the way these things will be stored in others' memories, will echo after we're gone.

Chapter One:
An Ambush of Mercy

At the age of 48 I hadn't been backpacking since my only daughter's birth almost six years earlier. I decided that rather than go to the Raweh Wilderness in Colorado, the wilderness I'd backpacked in several times, I'd try the Pecos Wilderness near Santa Fe, New Mexico. I wasn't planning a rugged adventure. There was a Creativity and Madness psychotherapy conference in Santa Fe, and I was feeling a bit stale and too settled after seven years of marriage and too many years living in Chicago, so I figured I needed a mildly risk-free bout of solitude and nature, followed by a curated tour of madness and creativity.

Because I hadn't been in high altitude in several years, I hired a wrangler so I could horseback up into a remote spot, and then he'd take the horses back to the ranch and leave me to my solitude. Once I got there and my body acclimated to the altitude, I'd be able to eventually hike my way downhill back to the ranch.

But my backpacking experience in the Raweh, and knowing I'd have a guide on the way up, had made me careless. Instead of getting a topo map, I took only a general map of the area. I hadn't known that unlike the Raweh, the Pecos trails were much more difficult to follow. Later I learned, too late, that by August several backpackers had already gotten lost there, one of them never found. I drove to the ranch, parked my car, and met the wrangler, who was a good half foot taller than me with a handlebar mustache and a genuine cowboy hat.

"How used are you to riding a horse?" he asked.

"Well," I said, "if you've got a horse named El Diablo and one named Old Fred, I'd be better off on Old Fred."

So he packed up Old Fred and we started out. The trip up took several hours; it would have taken less time but Old Fred kept stopping to nibble grass. Knowing I had a fairly useless map, I'd intended to memorize as much of the trail as I could on the way up, but we never took a trail. When we finally got to a high isolated area, we unpacked Old Fred, and as I got off him and his swayback slowly eased back into a straight line, I realized that I had strained a groin muscle. The wrangler pointed in the distance and told me I could pick up the trail headed back somewhere over there, and then he left. I set up my tent and went to look for some water and a walking stick: my pulled muscle was aching badly. Instead of exploring the area, the smartest thing was to stay still and heal as much as I could for the hike back in a few days. But for the first time on my backpacking trips, the altitude bothered me: I had a dull headache, I felt vaguely depressed, I had difficulty concentrating, I had no appetite, and that night I slept poorly. I was suffering the most insidious effect of altitude sickness: I wasn't thinking clearly, and I didn't realize it.

I still felt headachy and lethargic the next day. The solitude didn't feel good. Maybe it was being a father, maybe it was the altitude sickness, maybe the unfamiliarity of the Pecos, the planned shortness of the trip, the enforced limited mobility, the lack of adventure and effort on the trip up, but this trip wasn't doing anything for me. I spent one more sleepless night in my tent and the next morning, still feeling crummy, I decided to leave. I packed up and managed to find the trail. Unlike the Raweh trails, this one was indistinct. For over an hour I hiked gradually downhill, losing the trail occasionally, but as long as I kept heading downhill I knew that I was heading in the right direction. Then the trail started curving and heading back up. That shouldn't have happened, but my map was no help so I kept walking. My groin injury started aching worse, and it was getting toward late afternoon, the time of thunderstorms, so I couldn't afford to stop. I had to find my way out. Theoretically, every trail leads somewhere, but when you're backpacking in the wilderness, desperation can lead into deeper trouble.

At about three in the afternoon, the thunderstorm started moving in, just as the trail abruptly ended at a large high mountain meadow, surrounded on every side with forest. The trail just stopped. If I'd had a topo map I could have figured out where it picked up again—and more important where I was—but now I didn't have a clue. I just knew that I should have been a few thousand feet below if I were to get out of the wilderness before night. So the best move was to pitch my tent before the storm hit and somehow, hopefully, figure out the next day where I was. Nearly out of water, I put my small mess kit pot outside to catch the rain and hail. I didn't sleep well that night. I kept waking up and looking at my useless map, hoping to figure out *something* about where I was. It made no sense to go back down the same trail, so the next morning I used branches to spell out a Help sign that might be visible from the air, and then I limped all around the pasture.

Eventually I saw a barely noticeable notch in a tree trunk on the far side of the meadow. A trailhead. I estimated from my useless rough map that it would lead to a campground about three hours away. Still uncertain it was the right trail, but reminding myself that every trail eventually led somewhere, I decided to risk leaving my tent and most of my equipment: because of my groin injury I had to travel light. I left a note inside my tent explaining where I was going and struck out. That way, in case I was wrong or the aching muscle finally tore, a rescue team might find my tent, read the note and know roughly where to search.

Three hours later, finally down in the lower lands, I came to a shallow rivulet, not even deep enough to cover its stones. By now the mid-afternoon thunderclouds began massing again. I estimated that the campground was an hour or so downstream, and I had to make it there or I was in for a soaking and a steep temperature drop. But cliff bottoms started crowding the riverbank, forcing me to keep crisscrossing the river, which ran deeper and faster at each crossing. Finally, in the middle of the fourth or fifth crossing, I suddenly sunk to my waist, nearly lost my footing, and almost got swept downstream by the current. Frantic, I righted myself and fought my way ashore. What little I had in my backpack was now soaked and useless. I threw the backpack away, still thinking that the campground must be close.

Soon I was too exhausted to go any further, and I realized that I'd badly miscalculated: the campground couldn't be anywhere in this area, and I didn't have enough strength to backtrack through the river again: even if I made it back to my first crossing, where would I go from there? I'd finally run out of options: I remembered that one of the first rules when you're lost is to stay put so you and the rescue team don't keep missing each other, so I decided to make my stand and do without food, shelter or dry clothing until hopefully someone found me. With the thunderstorm about to break wide open. I scrambled under a rocky overhang and squatted on my haunches, pressing myself tightly against the cliff. As I crouched under the overhang, I wrote a goodbye note for my wife and my daughter Alex on the back of a wallet-sized photo of Alex that I always carried. Water streamed down the cliff and found a crack in the overhang, spattering the back of my neck. The dry spot between the blowing rain in front of me and the dripping water behind me kept shrinking. Piles of hail formed at my feet.

When the rain stopped I knew that now there were only three things to focus on: stay hydrated, avoid further injuries, and keep warm at night, trying to survive long enough for someone to maybe find me. Eventually the wrangler would report me missing because I'd left my car there. I went higher up a hill so any rescue team could more easily spot me, or I could spot them, and I collected a pile of pinion branches for warm cover at night. I spent the next few days limping down to the river to drink and limping back to the top of the hill so a search plane could spot me, knowing that there might not even be any search plane, and then making my way back down to the river for water again. But I was weakening rapidly. The first round trip took over an hour. The trip the next day took almost four. My hands developed blisters from clutching my walking stick, my feet were torn, and I had to start easing myself up and down parts of the hill on my butt.

As exhaustion and exposure took over, I began seeing and hearing things. Drinking from the river, I vividly saw myself sitting a little way down the bank, calmly watching me drink. "I'll only be a minute," I reassured myself, communicating telepathically but actually hearing my voice. "Take your time, I'm okay," I called back to me. Several times I heard automobile horns or barking dogs and imagined that a road or a cabin was just beyond the trees. My mind started drifting. Climbing across a rock wall toward a cactus I intended to eat—a stupid move—I told myself to concentrate, knowing that if I injured myself I'd die more quickly, but I watched a hawk soar across the sky and climbed mindlessly past the cactus. Then I forgot where I had put my flannel shirt—I'd hung it on a branch to dry. Inside the pocket was the goodbye note I'd written. Next I couldn't locate my bedding cache of dry branches, and while I was searching desperately for it—if I couldn't stay warm at night, I wouldn't survive—I got caught in another late afternoon hailstorm. Suddenly it was dusk, the temperature had plummeted, and I squatted by a pinion tree shivering in my damp T-shirt and torn jeans, rubbing my hands and realizing that I'd gone as far as I could go. I knew that that evening I would slip into a coma. I felt calm about dying, almost like a novitiate, and hoped only that I wouldn't suffer too much before I lost consciousness.

Then I thought about Alex. I imagined her experiencing my going on a short vacation and never returning—her father suddenly disappearing without a goodbye, forever. Could she ever trust any relationship again? At that moment, I would have given anything to appear to her for just one minute, just to reassure her that although I was going to die, sometimes she would still be able to close her eyes and see me. I'd always accused my own father of caring more about himself than about me, and I suppose in the back of my mind, ever since Alex had been born I'd assumed that if it ever came down to deciding between my living or dying, I'd have chosen life because I'd want to enjoy watching her grow up and wanting her to know me. But now I knew that I wanted to stay alive only to reassure her, to leave her some kind of security that would help her through the rest of her childhood. It wasn't at all about my wanting her to remember me. I understood, in the gulf inside my chest, that her world would no longer feel safe. She would always fear loss. I thought of her flinching whenever she began to feel love.

Then an amazing thing happened: I saw her face floating in the thin mountain air like a hologram. Just about ten feet away, it was so clear that I watched her expression slowly melt from innocence into fear and then into sadness. Squatting underneath the pinion tree, still wringing my hands, I squeezed my eyes shut and shook my head no, trying to shake off what I saw. But as her face faded, I realized that my hands were no longer wringing. They'd begun rubbing, as if on their own they were trying to warm themselves, and then I consciously began to rub them more briskly. I understood, for the first time in my life, that as her father, I didn't have the right to let myself die. "I'm not going to die," I muttered aloud. "I'm not going to die."

I took my knife from my belt sheathe and began digging a trench, muttering over and over, "I'm not going to die," until the meaning of the words dissolved into repetitive sound, like a mantra or a child's babble. I worked steadily, completely focused. Determined to use everything to survive, I placed every rock and stone that I dug out just beyond the growing pile of dirt, building a water and wind break alongside the edge of my trench. Finally, I had my trench dug— a little over a foot wide and a foot deep. I climbed in and raised my knees just enough to fit, the back of my head resting against the tree and, yes, it occurred to me that it looked like a grave. I scooped all the dug out dirt on top of me and packed it firmly, covering everything from my collarbone down, except for my scooping arm. Then I thrust my arm into the last loose pile of dirt and waited to see whether the dirt would keep me warm enough when my body cooled from the exertion.

It didn't. I soon began to shiver, and I knew I had to keep it under control. Shivering, the body's short-term attempt to keep warm, uses up precious energy; it's the beginning of a spiral into fatal hypothermia. Then I remembered my yoga from over 20 years ago, when I used to stave off depression by lighting a candle, turning out all the lights in my apartment and losing myself inside my stretching and breathing. I began deep breathing and chanting, "*Aauuummmmmm.*" Soon the shivering slowed, then stopped, and I began to feel warmer, then actually warm. I continued deep breathing and chanting; eventually I found the flow, and soon it actually took less energy to continue chanting than to stop.

I always had this problem when I backpacked. Each night by the time the stars came fully out, it was too cold to lie on my back and stare up at them. Almost every night I had ever spent in the high mountains, burrowed into my warm sleeping bag, I'd regretted not going outside the tent, lying on my back and staring up into the vast night sky until a pleasant dizziness took hold. But when I knew I would survive on that midsummer night in the Pecos Wilderness, lying packed in dirt, breathing in the night air and chanting out toward the stars, I came as close to perfection as I will ever come. I was safe and in deep peace. Up in the night sky, a small plane buzzed and blinked, like a blind angel. He would not be able to see me, but at that moment it didn't matter: the plane, the stars, me, were all parts of a great panorama.

They found me the next afternoon through an extraordinary piece of luck. I had staggered down to the river at the exact moment a search team was walking along the opposite bank, calling my name. We couldn't see each other, but we were just close enough so I could hear my name over the rushing river. I *knew* it was real, that I wasn't imagining it like I'd imagined the automobile horns, and I knew that I had time and energy for one good shout. I took a deep breath. To have your life come down to one breath is an exquisite experience. I shouted, "Here!" and suddenly four people burst out of the brush, scrambled down the bank and thrashed through the river, setting off smoke flares and shouting into radios. It was like an ambush of mercy. I rose and fell into someone's arms. "Oh, man," I said, and I saw with dull surprise that he had tears in his eyes.

Later some people insisted that God saved me, but I never bought it. Instead, for several years I called it love, which was close enough to grace. Like God, love has millions of admirers, worshippers, believers, doubters and zealots and more often than not, just like the concept of God, love is misused, misinterpreted, wielded as a weapon or an excuse and honored by idolatry. For years I didn't tell Alex that I had stayed alive because of her. I feared that it would put too much of a burden on her, compelling her to live her life and develop her self because she'd feel she owed it to *me*. So

I kept the secret close to my heart, which I believe is where we should hold on to something sacred. Over the years though, I discovered I had had a different reason for surviving.

We touch this kind of experience only a few times in our lives, and when it happens, if we hold it right, the meaning that flows from it continues echoing and evolving.

CHAPTER TWO:
THE NAME'S THE SAME

I've always had this ambivalent relationship with intimacy and it goes back to Aunt Gert, who I never knew, never even met. She was some secondary or tertiary aunt in the family constellation. I never tried to find out anything more about her. You'd think I would have been a little curious because I was named after her: Jewish custom said parents should give their newborn a name that began with the first letter of the name of the most recent family member who'd died, and that was the misty Gert. My parents always claimed they hadn't even thought about Gary Cooper, who was then at the height of his career, a handsome cultural icon of high moral rectitude. It took me years to realize that giving me his name had probably not been the unaware act my parents claimed, and that they'd decided to spell Garry with two r's as a way to soothe their own vague misgivings.

But the different spelling failed to insulate me. At the start of every semester in grammar school the teacher would call each student's name, and I'd have already done the alphabetical calculation: I'd come right after Brian Cohen. She'd call out Garry Cooper and the class would laugh. Usually the teacher did too. Try saying "Here" while everyone's laughing at your name.

For years, whenever someone introduced me I braced for the joke. There were two kinds of people I met—the small minority who didn't say anything about my name when they heard it, and those who thought they could say something witty that I hadn't heard over and over, again and again. In other words, people I was willing to like and people who would have to work hard and long before I might have anything further to do with them.

I once thought about printing up a card with just three sentences on it:

I thought you were dead.
Where's your horse?
I saw you in *High Noon*

and every time someone said one of those things, I'd hand them the card and walk away without saying a word, letting it slowly dawn on them that they had just said something utterly predictable and not clever. Although these three comments were the most common, I've also heard, probably hundreds of times: "I thought you were taller." Or, "Are you the *real* Gary Cooper?" Some people hummed the theme from *High Noon*. Then there were the ones who said, "I bet you get lots of jokes about your name." I found it a bit easier to forgive these people; at least the line had a tinge of sympathy. As for its variant, "I'm not going to make a joke about your name," my silent response was always, "You just did, you asshole."

I recognize it's too simplistic to blame my name for having injected such introversion into my personality. As a therapist, I know about the tangled interplay between nature and nurture—the roles of genes, parents, siblings, and life experiences. Nevertheless even today I still internally flinch when I hear my name. I've never found a good way to respond to people laughing or joking about my name. Smiling good-naturedly means participating in my own abasement. Scowl, and I worry about getting tagged as a bad sport, over-sensitive. My name never feels like me.

When I was about six years old, my parents decided it would be a good idea to get me on *The Name's the*

Same, a national television show hosted by Robert Q. Lewis. (I wondered whether the Q hid something embarrassing for Lewis. It turns out, according to *Wikipedia,* that he added the Q himself, because Robert Lewis was such a generic name). National television!—and I'd make some money too. *That'd* help me feel better about my name. The premise of *The Name's the Same* was pure 50's game show simplicity. Someone comes on with a famous name, the studio and at-home audience see the name flash on the screen, and the panel, who can ask only yes or no questions, tries to guess it. For verification, the producers requested a copy of my birth certificate, and they disqualified me because my name was spelled with two r's. (In a further irony, to this day about a third of the people I know—including people who have already seen my name spelled out, often several times—spell it with one r. Now they sometimes blame it on autocorrect, but it's been happening long before computers).

When I learned that I was unfit to appear on *The Name's the Same,* I felt disappointed. But I recently came across a clip of the show which featured a six-year old child guest named Bill Cullen—the same name as one of the show's panelists, ha ha. The panel's questions always conflated the guest with the "real" person, so when a panelist asked him if he was a ladies' man, the audience laughed uproariously. I watched the kid closely. Young Bill Cullen could only smile in embarrassed confusion, an unwilling accomplice in the laughter. (I also discovered an additional level of irony about the "real" Bill Cullen: he always sat behind a desk so the national TV audience wouldn't know he'd been crippled by polio).

Anger is the conjoined twin of shame. The other day at a party, my host introduced me to someone and, sure enough, he said, "Wait until I tell my wife I met Gary Cooper." I smiled—my version of the Uncle Tom shuffle—while fantasizing that if he had a heart attack and fell to the floor right in front of me, I'd pretend I didn't know CPR and stand helplessly over his purpling face. With that pleasant reverie inside my head, I walked over to the drinks. But then I realized that if by some stroke of divine justice he *did* have a heart attack, I'd probably turn back and give him CPR just because it's the right thing to do. I imagined him lying on the ground, me giving him chest compressions. He comes to, and as the paramedics carry him away he looks back at me and says, "Wait till I tell people I was saved by Gary Cooper."

24

Chapter Three:
Naomi and Herb

My parents were almost complete opposites, and I admired and disparaged the wrong qualities in each. My extraverted father embarrassed me, and I mistook my mother's reticence to show emotion as strength. We create caricatures of our parents. Parents' identities are like quicksilver: after they die, their identity shatters and pieces of it pass on to their survivors.

In the earliest memory of my life, I am three, maybe four years old, feverish, lying on my back on a couch and Mrs. Wallace, our family's once every two weeks cleaning lady, is patting my forehead with a cool washcloth. My entire memory is of the couch, the washcloth and Mrs. Wallace's eyes; I have no recollection of what her face looked like. My mother, always efficient, must have been somewhere in the small apartment.

Naomi believed that because emotions dwelled in the dangerous province of spontaneity they shouldn't readily be expressed or shared. She sometimes smiled and laughed, but not too loudly or too long. The apex of her emotional range was pleasure, the bottom, acceptance. Her tears and joy were secret things.

Herb, on the other hand, an anxious overweight man, met social situations head on. He once surprised me by insisting he was a shy person, and it took me years to understand that, because no one who knew Herb would have described him as shy. When he laughed, he often liked to say, "Who has more fun than people?" He had an almost meteoric rise from Cub Scoutmaster to Boy Scoutmaster, and then into volunteer work as some Boy Scout District muckety-muck. (I, on the other hand, didn't much like Cub or Boy Scouts. I often felt I was in them because of *his* needs). It took me years to understand that the way he showed up and dove into activities was a cover for his anxious insecurity.

When I was about 10 years old, our family saw Dean Martin and Jerry Lewis onstage at the Chicago Theatre. We sat in the balcony, and at some point my father's loud laughter spread like wildfire, even down to the main floor, until I wondered whether Martin and Lewis were pleased because the audience was laughing so much or annoyed that my father's laughter messed up their timing and overpowered their material. That was just one of hundreds of times when I vowed to not be like him. My mother never made a fool of herself. The few times my father got angry at her, she went silent so his anger quickly melted into embarrassment.

Until I went into therapy in my mid-20's I believed that my mother epitomized strength and my father weakness, and so significant parts of myself never breathed deeply. I only sang out loud when I was hitchhiking on country highways, camping alone in the mountains, or showering when no one else was home (even then I'd occasionally worry that an upstairs neighbor might hear me). As a teenager and for years after, when everyone sang the national anthem at Chicago Cubs games, I stayed silent, pretending that my silence was a protest against Vietnam, Johnson, Nixon, capitalism, nationalism, imperialism, whatever. I never chanted at anti-war demonstrations, not even when I threw a rock and smashed a state trooper's windshield.

Psychologists debate whether our personalities are influenced more by our biological template or by how we're raised and what we encounter. My grandparents' and parents' personalities lent weight to either hypothesis. My maternal grandfather Louie had to sneak out of Lithuania when he was about 17 years old, leaving behind his mother and father forever. Louie's father, a tailor for the Russian army, had learned from a friendly officer that the army was about to conscript Louie. Because Jews in the Russian army were cannon fodder, the next day Louie began a clandestine journey to Bremen, Germany where he embarked for America on the Koeningen Louise, never to see his mother and father or hear their voices again. Louie's name was actually Itzik Leib Lewin. When he arrived at Ellis Island, an immigration official asked him his name and Itzik, not understanding English and terrified of men in uniforms, assumed the official had asked what ship he'd arrived on. He said "Louise," and at that moment Itzik Leib Lewin ceased to exist and Louis Levin started a new life in America. A quarter century after his death, I discovered his embarkation card among his papers, searched in vain for a Louis Levin who landed at Ellis Island, and thus pieced together the story of Itzik Leib and the Koeningen Louise. I told my mother, but it didn't interest her in the slightest. After all, what's so important about a name change? Louie, mild nearly unto invisibility, never said a bad word about anyone.

When he was especially content, he sang tuneless notes. No one, as far as I know, ever saw him angry. Even his death was perfectly undramatic: he died in an instant playing pinochle at the local park field house.

Louie perched high up in the air in one pan of the balance scale of his marriage, while my grandmother Zvicki (his first cousin, incidentally—any port in a storm) sat solidly in the other pan. Everything about Zvicki's countenance communicated that we are born to endure in a difficult world. A woman with two massive arms and a mole on her chin, she cruised around their apartment like a battleship. My ten-year old brother, not afraid of anything, once saw her coming angrily after him and ran outside coatless into subzero temperature, headed he knew not where. My mother insisted that Zvicki had been a gentle, kind mother, but once, years after Zvicki's death, my third grade daughter Alex asked her what some of her happy childhood memories were. "I can't think of any," my mother said, without regret.

The eyes of my paternal grandpa Sam were distorted behind thick glasses, so I never clearly saw his eyes. Like Louie, he never raised his voice nor expressed an opinion, unlike his wife Helen who used to chase after my father and his brothers swinging at them with the heavy cord from an iron. The one time Sam dared to express himself, he did it indirectly; then Helen found out about his affair and made him pay for it the rest of his life. Helen, a hellion, fancied herself a genius who'd been cheated by the world. She and Sam ran a catering business, and Helen bitterly insisted all her life that because a rival caterer took credit for her invention of Bavarian Jello, she'd had to work like a dog just to make ends meet.

Naomi and Herb were an ill-suited well-suited match who balanced each other. But when my father, terminally bed-ridden and half-crazed with metastasized cancer and opiates, complained to my mother that the speakers under his bed were making too much noise, instead of removing the imaginary speakers she insisted they didn't exist, until they were both shouting at each other. Several months before he died, my efficient mother, knowing that he would never need his suits again, gave away all his clothes to charity. She saved his ugliest suit for his burial, reasoning that he'd have to wear *something* in his coffin, and not even a poor person would want that suit. A few years after his death, my mother, at the age of 76, had a mastectomy, and she did not use the morphine pump by her bedside even once.

Even when kids think they know who their parents are, the depth of their knowing is like looking at the moon. One July Fourth evening when I was about seven years old, I sat in the grass by a river watching the fireworks, my father standing above me. In between the skyrockets, I looked up at him and watched him staring into the sky, his face silhouetted against the trees and sky, and I remember briefly wondering for the first time in my life what he was thinking about.

From the time I was about nine, once a month in the summer Herb and I went fishing at the Chain of Lakes, 60 miles north of our Chicago apartment. Accompanying him felt at least partly like a duty, waking up early, watching him on chilly mornings as he obsessively, compulsively, slowly packed everything neatly into the car trunk, half of which we never used. He always dreamed of owning a boat. Nothing big, no Cadillac yacht or Jaguar speedboat, just something of his own so he could travel across all the lakes in the Chain in something other than a rented rowboat with a putt-putt motor. We fished for bluegills, crappies and striped bass; our catches weighed ounces, not pounds. The large northern pikes and muskies were for *sportsmen*—too big for our rods and light tackle, but you never knew, maybe one day.... Nevertheless, he purchased a fishing net just in case we accidentally snagged one and somehow managed to pull it alongside us. The only time he ever used the net was when he and a friend got silly on two beers apiece. My father put the net on his head and pretended to be a baseball umpire calling out balls and strikes.

Eventually he managed to buy his own 4 ½ horsepower motor. It was barely more powerful than the rented motor, but it was *his*. On Sundays we'd drive to the Chain, lug the motor from the car trunk to the clunky rented boat, attach it to the rear—I mean the *stern*—and motor slowly out, looking for a sheltered spot where the speedboats weren't zooming past and rocking us in their wakes. I remember one afternoon sitting in the front of the rowboat, the weight of my father and of the heavy motor in the rear elevating the front—the *prow*—higher. When we left the shelter of the bay and reached the open water, I turned my face into the light spray and wind, pulled my baseball cap down low on my forehead so it wouldn't blow off, and imagined I was a square-jawed Captain, scanning the horizon.

By the time I got to high school, I hated going fishing with him. But he'd aged, and his excuse for dragging me along was that needed me to carry the motor from our basement shed to his car trunk and from his car to the boat. I soon found a way out of the trap. I had a summer job at a factory, and one day I walked past the security guard with five big empty cardboard boxes loaded onto a two wheel hand truck.

"What's in those boxes?" the guard asked.

"They're just empties," I said. "Our family's moving."

He checked the boxes and waved me past, and I had the hand truck stolen.

My father loved nature and camping, though we experienced them only at nearby state parks where you were always around other campers, some of whom didn't even have tents but camper shells on their pickup trucks. We were the most contemptuous of them. They called that *camping*? We had a heavy canvas tent with an umbrella pole, room enough for my father, sister and me, plus our suitcases. (My mother, who feared anything more feral and natural than a housefly or a potted plant, stayed home).

Herb wasn't a critical person, just that his anxiety seldom allowed him to leave things well enough alone. Loading the car trunk or getting the tent set up were never pleasant. I was supposed to help him but his anxiously impatient instructions were always vague, like, "Hold that" or, "Give me that." I seldom had any idea what the that was, and whenever I guessed wrong or stood helplessly by he'd get annoyed. He desperately wanted to be an outdoorsman, and outdoorsmen got their tents set up quickly and easily.

Even our camp meals had to be a production. My little sister and I would have been happier with hot dogs on a stick and bags of potato chips. Once he decided to build a Dutch oven over the fire pit and make biscuits from scratch. They took forever and, like most biscuits, turned out pretty unremarkable. To this day I've never bothered to learn what Dutch oven actually is.

The closest he came to achieving woodsmanship was on the chilly mornings. While my sister and I stayed in our warm sleeping bags trying to delay emerging as long as possible, he was already outside, had filled a plastic basin with cold water from the pump, taken off his shirt, stripped down to his undershorts and thoroughly washed himself from head to toes. That and his stentorian snoring epitomized a manliness I was so far from embodying that trying to get there didn't interest me at all. (At home, my mother sometimes got so annoyed at his snoring that she'd go sleep in the dry bathtub. She could have slept much better on the living room couch, but then he wouldn't have known how much she suffered from his snoring).

When I was 22, I left Chicago for my first great adventure, to start a new life in New Orleans, with no job and almost no money. The Sixties supported adventures like that. The night before I left, my father drove me to my apartment and as we turned down my block I wanted to already be out of the car in order to avoid a goodbye that was irrevocably headed toward cliche. He doubleparked the car, we sat awkwardly for a second, and in a sudden rush he hugged me and I heard myself saying, "You always make me cry." I say that I heard myself saying it because that's how I experienced it; I had absolutely no idea I was going to say it and had no idea what I meant, because it was demonstrably untrue.

When I returned to Chicago from New Orleans seven months later, my father and I continued drifting further apart. The fault was mine. I had no idea nor interest about what to do with a BA in English Lit, let alone with the rest of my life, so I drove a cab, which made my father worry. But what bothered my father was often a point of pride for me. Later I decided to start backpacking by myself in the Rockies. It seems so obvious now, but I didn't realize it was a way to escape my father's anxious shadow, and show him up by proving I could camp in *real* nature.

Here are three stories about my mother. In my mid-twenties I went into therapy and finally began to learn that my deficiencies in connecting with others weren't because of any innate flaws about who I "really" was. So I decided to take her out to lunch and have a meaningful conversation. Her restaurant lunches with friends were always at the same delis, where they ordered the usual things of middle-aged, middle-class ladies: a tuna sandwich or a Hollywood salad—a piece of lettuce with a scoop of cottage cheese on it, topped by a canned peach or pear. Maybe I hadn't learned as much in therapy as I should have, because I took her to my favorite Vietnamese restaurant. She couldn't locate anything recognizable on the menu, but surely every restaurant could make a grilled cheese sandwich, and she didn't hide her disdain when the ignorant waiter had no idea what that was. I told her that lemon grass chicken was a little like chop suey, but one taste convinced her that they were so dumb they didn't even know how to make good chop suey.

Twenty-five years later, after I'd had another round of therapy, she told me about a conversation the previous week with three of her friends. "All they did was brag about their children," she said. "I finally told them, 'Well, there must be something wrong with me because *my* children are very mediocre.'" Instead of being hurt or insulted, I was amused. I understood that her point wasn't about me being mediocre but that *she* wasn't one of those people who always bragged about their children. Nevertheless, did she have to say *very* mediocre?

Not long after that, her old friend Evelyn, who she hadn't seen since Ev and Mort had moved halfway across the country six years ago, came in for a brief visit. Evelyn's daughter had just had a baby, and Evelyn dug into her purse to pull out a photo of her first grandchild, needlessly asking, "Would you like to see a picture of him?"

"I don't need to," my mother replied. "Every baby looks the same." My mother told me that Evelyn's offended reaction just showed how touchy Evelyn was.

When Herb died my mother had her own name and date of birth carved on the stone alongside his, reasoning that because prices would only go up, it made sense to have as much of the engraving as possible done ahead of time. When she died, we honored her request for the most modest service available, no visitation or chapel. Although I had delivered a eulogy at my father's service, I didn't deliver one for my mother. She'd had a lifelong habit of unenthusiastically receiving gifts, and so I paradoxically gave her a final gift of not giving her a final gift.

She left me a mixed emotional legacy. I appreciate intimate moments more than *she* was able to appreciate them, and although I occasionally feel like kicking them away, I often catch myself in time. Her thorny love taught me at an early age to anticipate people's reactions, a useful skill for a therapist and a hunter of love. It's also a survival skill: someone wandering in the desert had better figure out whether those shimmering trees near the horizon are a mirage or an actual oasis. Chase after the illusion or ignore the oasis and you die of thirst.

As for my father, before he got cancer I decided to get closer to him. Herb had given up camping and fishing many years ago. I learned there was a state park in Wisconsin's nearby Door County where instead of setting up your tent close to other families and their cars and RVs, you could hike a third of a mile to a secluded campsite. I decided to give my father a gift, a return for him to nature and to camping, and—although I didn't admit it to myself—to prove to him that even though I never could help him set up that damn leviathan canvas tent or cook a fancy camp meal, I could show him how to *really* camp. We went on a warm summer day, and to ease his load I carried my 2-man mountain tent, sleeping pads and cookware and everything else I could pack and strap to my backpack frame. When we woke up in the morning, my father, who'd once embraced chilly weather and cold water bathing, said he hadn't slept well because he'd been so cold. We left that afternoon even though we'd reserved the site for two nights.

Maybe my father had occasionally dreamed about getting to the rugged kind of nature I came to know, of the glacial lakes, the solitude, pure air and quiet that exists only at high altitudes. All those times when my father and his motor took us to the inlets of the crowded lake, I assumed he was just focused on getting us to a decent fishing spot. As he steered his 4 ½ horsepower motor—the shadow of his boat dream—it never occurred to me that he might be having his own fantasies or brooding on his own unrealized dreams. My father's unspoken yearnings interested me so little that, except for that Fourth of July evening on the banks of the Fox River, I didn't even know they existed. Beyond his wanting a boat, I never found out what they were.

As for my mother, as I grew older I used to amuse myself by thinking of her as a Jewish Buddhist: she lived a mostly calm life, and if you observed her from enough of a distance, denial of emotion looked the same as acceptance. So here's the koan she left for me. You have two ropes, denial and acceptance, knotted together in the middle. You pull on the ends and the knot disappears.

Chapter Four:
Weeds in the Sidewalk Cracks

I was in my thirties when my father had his cancerous prostate taken out, but we never talked about the operation, what it meant to him, how it might affect his spirits, his life. It took me years to understand that my father's prostate cancer hadn't been just another depot in his life. Instead, a genetic switch had wrenched his life onto a different track.

Because that was one of the cancers that has stalked my family, I began submitting to the indignity of a prostate exam after I passed 50, feeling as foolish each time as if I'd been caught wearing a bicycle helmet. I took a baseline PSA test that first year and when I was 58, just for the hell of it, I took another one. The blood test showed a suspicious leap in my PSA count. Nothing to worry about, the doc said, PSA tests were occasionally inaccurate. But when the second results came back the same, he sent me for a biopsy.

I expected the biopsy would exonerate me. My father's cancer hadn't been detected until he was around 65, and I led a much healthier life. So when the urologist called and said I had cancer, I'm not usually into denial but I wondered for a moment whether there'd been a lab error. Then I made room in my head for the sudden new reality. Cancer. I felt more shame than fear. After I made the emergency appointment to return to the urologist, feeling dazed I walked to the computer for distraction and saw an email from my friend Sheldon, complaining about something.

"You think you've got troubles," I emailed back. "I just found out I have prostate cancer."

A minute later he called. I didn't want to pick up the phone, like when you're ringing the doorbell for your first date, and you want to run and hide before a parent answers. He asked me what the doctor said and, surprised, I found that I couldn't speak. "Give me a second," I said. I took a few deep breaths to steady my voice.

Not showing any overt signs of cancer or feeling any effects, I nevertheless began to see myself as sickly and ashamed. The flu or a broken limb are fine: they're temporary, so you can feel sick or incapacitated and sanguine about accepting sympathy because you know the healing will begin quickly. A broken limb usually carries an interesting story. I was once on crutches for several weeks, and for all the hassle and discomfort, there was a motorcycle accident behind it, a thing of manliness and glory. The crutches marked me as a warrior. Cancer made me feel pathetic, marked, inferior.

The urologist recommended implanting radioactive seeds. But a second opinion from one of the top urologist oncologists in the area recommended taking the prostate out. "If it's shown up this early it's most likely an aggressive cancer," he said, and in fact the biopsy showed a fair amount of it. The seeds weren't guaranteed to get at all the cancer in the prostate, the procedure carried a greater risk of incontinence, and if the cancer returned, I'd have to get a prostatectomy anyway, and then the scarring from the seeds could make post op incontinence and impotence more likely. A prostatectomy would let us see how much cancer there was (biopsies could give only good estimates) and whether the cancer had spread to the lymph nodes, in which case there'd be more decisions to make. The prostatectomy offered the best chance of getting ahead of the cancer and surviving, but the seeds offered the best chance of salvaging a normal sex life. Sex or death, the outcome of either not under warranty. I decided on the prostatectomy; I'd already had experience losing my sex life during droughts between relationships, and I figured I could endure that better than death.

When my father had his prostate operation, he came out of the anesthesia completely psychotic. For about 72 hours he raged and hallucinated, convinced he'd been kidnapped by Nazis who were holding him against his will. He kept ripping out his IV so they finally had to belt down his arms, which convinced him even more this was a Nazi prison camp disguised as a hospital. Because I refused his request to cut off his straps, he branded me a collaborator. Finally he turned strategic and called the nurse over. "Nurse," he said sweetly, "could you please cut this cheese that's on my arms?" When the nurse proved too smart to fall for that one, he called her a Nazi whore. Then he had me dial my brother-in-law and hold the phone by his head so he could talk.

"Jeff," he said, "I want you to come over to the hospital right away and bring a knife so you can cut this cheese off me."

"I'll be right over, Herb," Jeff said.

My father glared at me. "At least someone in this family has some fucking sense," he said.

After a lifetime of anxiety and insecurity, Herb finally found his voice in the hospital room: he raged magnificently against the Nazis, who represented everything and everyone who had ever held him down in his life. All night and the following day, glaring and raging, he struggled against the straps.

On his second day, he remained crazy but calmed down, and they took off his straps. My sister and I exchanged the kind of non sequiturs with him that pass for conversation with a psychotic person. Suddenly my father said we were being rude and embarrassing him. I asked why.

"Bob's been standing here and you two haven't even said hello to him."

I looked at the head of his bed, where Bob stood or sat or floated, and told my father that I was sorry I hadn't noticed him.

"Well, aren't you gonna say hello?"

I told Bob hi, and my father asked me what Bob had said.

"He...didn't say anything," I replied.

"What kind of expression's on his face?"

"Um, kind of blank."

Satisfied, my father leaned back on his pillow and closed his eyes.

"I feel like we're back tripping in the 60's," my sister said.

And that's how we formulated our theory about Sundown Syndrome, the temporary psychosis that sometimes affects older people after operations. We decided that this generation, because they hadn't had experiences with mind-altering substances, simply couldn't handle their meds. So when I woke up in my hospital bed after my operation and saw the chair halfway up the wall, I remained calm, telling myself this was merely the after effects of the anesthesia. Then I thought: but what if things remain this way? Lying flat on my back, I suddenly felt like I couldn't breathe. I called for a nurse, worried that if she didn't show fast, I'd die. Then I saw her standing with her feet on the wall, staring straight down at the floor where she was supposed to be.

"I know this is only the after effects of the anesthesia," I said, trying to keep my voice calm, "but it looks like you're standing on the wall. I can't breathe. Can you lift my head?"

"I'm right here," she said, suddenly by my bedside, pressing the button that raised my head and making my pillow more comfortable. I was luckier than my father. No Nazi, she was beautiful, and I loved her. When she went back toward the chair, she walked up the wall again.

"It looks like you're on the wall again," I said, and I drifted back into sleep, hoping that when I awakened everything would be in its proper place.

When I almost died in the Pecos Wilderness, I learned that I, like most people, have a much greater capacity to endure than I knew. When our nightmares finally arrive, we walk through them, step by step. Your world narrows when you come out of a major operation. The catheter. The drain in your side. The drip in your arm. The jerk in the other bed who thinks he's the most important person in the world. In your narrowed world you feel enormously grateful for small things. The sudden seep of painkiller into your veins. The hands and strong arms that lift you. The sponge bath. The nurse falling for it when you lie and say you had a bowel movement and that you'd forgotten her instructions and flushed the toilet. Your sense of time and distance narrows: you measure your progress in minutes and yards. The first slow walk down the hall, each step, your rolling IV bag and pole like a personal valet. A few evenings after I returned home, I took a walk to the park, just a block away, figuring that if I rested there, I could make the round trip. Exhausted when I reached the park, I sat on a bench, reached down, and popped open the valve on my small walking catheter bag, taking a piss in the park for the first time in my life without worrying about getting busted. Maybe I wanted to mark my territory, telling myself and the world that I'd returned.

On my next appointment, the doctor went over the pathology report. Like the biopsy, it showed that my cancer was on the borderline between medium and high risk. Although the cancer hadn't broken out of its tumor shape—a good sign—the tumor was more loose than compact—a bad sign. The looser tumor could have been an artifact not of a more advanced cancer but of the testosterone suppressant, which has a tendency to soften tumors, and that would be a good sign. Even though there was no sign of it having spread to my lymph nodes—which would have been an awful sign—if a few cells had spread there, they could have escaped detection, so the good sign wasn't great. The amount of cancer in the prostate moved me uncomfortably near high risk, a bad sign, but it wasn't close to the edge of the prostate, which was a good sign. The doctor recommended several years of hormone therapy, just as "insurance," he said. Sitting in the doctor's office, I realized I'd thought that I'd beaten the cancer or at least gotten so far ahead of it that by the time it returned I'd be old enough to die of some other natural cause. To have escaped cancer and then still have to deal with it.... I needed time to think, and the doctor told me there was no rush: I had some time.

Although I mostly believe that none of these things guarantee a cancer-free life or cure, I nevertheless have something in common with cancer patients who put their faith in a god, macrobiotics, clean living, karma, or positive thinking: we cling to something that we hope might maybe work for us. I still occasionally think that instead of diverting my energy toward false promises, believing in nothing makes more energy available to my immune system. When the chips are down, our backs against the wall, and the Visigoths storming the gates, we all clutch for superstitious hope.

Following my surgery, I began seeing a Chinese acupuncturist and herbalist. Every two weeks he gave me a few baggies of moldy and necrotic looking roots, fungi and herbs that I brewed into a vile tea. "Dr. Feng," I'd say for the next two years, "I'm worried about my cancer coming back." He'd look at my tongue, ask about my energy, sleep and urination, feel my pulses—in Chinese medicine, you compare the pulses in several places on each wrist and feel not just their rate but the relative strengths of their beats and which areas of each pulse are strongest—and he'd say, "No worry, I think you be all right," and I'd feel a little more safe. For several years, every time he felt my pulses I scanned his face for a worried expression, however slight. It's difficult to see the difference between concentration and worry. Whenever he said everything was fine, I listened hard to his voice, trying to detect a slight tremor of insincerity. I wished he'd leave off the "I think" and just make the unqualified assertion. For years afterward, sometimes when I realized I'd stopped worrying, I'd wonder whether now that my guard was down the cancer would take advantage of this opportunity to strike again. Even now I sometimes try to think that the new hairs sprouting in my nose and ears are natural, a sign that my body, feeing the imperative to grow, is doing it with hair rather than cancer cells. But maybe it's a bad sign, that cells are multiplying out of control and it's only a matter of time before the cancerous cells start up again too, weeds cracking through the sidewalk

Mortality aside, fear's the main thing about cancer. It's not just shameful but *scary.* Your body's not fighting an outside invader; it's turned against you. You are being attacked from the inside. This helps explain why everyone uses the metaphor of *battling* cancer. In the face of threat, we're supposed to summon up our courage to *fight* the invader.

When we feel our survival is threatened, we react by fighting, fleeing, or freezing. We've learned to put values on those primitive strategies as though they're some measurement of our courage and cunning: the lion fights; the rabbit runs for cover; the prairie dog freezes to escape detection. Irrationally, we think that only fighting is noble. But sometimes running in order to live another day under more auspicious conditions is a noble strategy. And we don't give enough respect to the almost delicious thrill of marshaling all your willpower to freeze, turning yourself into a pressure cooker that contains your feelings. Fighting might be like premature ejaculation, and who says there's anything noble about *that*? Being temperamentally disposed toward negotiation, which is an amalgamation of fighting, fleeing and freezing, I naturally endorse that method. Ultimately, every one of us, whether we have cancer or not, runs cost-benefit analyses, balancing how high a price we want to pay for how much time and breathing room. We do it with jobs, relationships, diseases, and treatment decisions.

For several weeks I pondered what to do about the hormone therapy. The thought of losing my muscles, some bone density, some short-term memory, and my libido for several years seemed almost as bad as dying of cancer. I'd chosen the prostatectomy over the seeds mostly because I wanted to be around for Alex—the lesson I'd learned and the vow I'd made in the Pecos. But now I decided that most of my work was done. In a year she'd be off to college. And hormone therapy,

I feared, would render me a much more irrelevant, maybe pathetic father, a shadow, a caricature. Better dead than white bread. Still, as friends kept reminding me, the notion that my work as a father had finished was more melodramatic than true, so I should choose more certain longevity. Finally I talked with a nurse friend, told her I was leaning against doing the hormone therapy, but couldn't quite make up my mind.

"If you don't do the hormone therapy and the cancer returns a few years from now," Gayle asked, "would you regret your decision?"

I knew immediately that I wouldn't regret it. It was time to choose living well over hanging around.

Not long after I made my decision, I was helping Alex with an AP English paper, and she asked if I was still seeing Dr. Feng. "You're worried I'll die before you're through with college and I won't be able to help you with your papers," I said, laughing. She laughed too, a little guiltily and told me that wasn't the only reason she'd asked. Cancer was just something in our lives, and it would be from now on.

PART TWO:
KICKING THE CAN DOWN THE ROAD

The Allure of Indeterminateness

If you don't know where you're heading, it can help to not worry so much about it. Call it the indeterminate cure for indeterminateness. Somewhere in the back of your mind you may occasionally fear that not worrying is just a temporary palliative that may even lead to even more trouble, but you can always tell yourself that temporariness can last a long, long time, and who knows what might be around the next bend? If you die tomorrow, in your last moment would you be disappointed that you hadn't gotten to where you were headed, or satisfied you'd made an effort, or would you kick yourself in the ass for having wasted so much time trying to get somewhere that will now be forever beyond your reach?

Chapter Five: New Orleans:
Mecca for the Dispossessed
and Dreamers

By supporting my defiance, the Sixties and early Seventies both nourished and stunted me. There were plenty of important things to oppose: Vietnam, conventional middle-class values, and a fierce belief that my parents' ideas about what adults should do would never lead anywhere meaningful. Marijuana, hallucinogens and the great Boomer demographic bulge fueled new perspectives, and my defiance overpowered any thoughts about working *toward* something, But when I wasn't reaping the excitement of the times and experimenting, I often felt adrift, confused, and depressed.

A BA in English had not prepared me for any career. (Though in retrospect it nurtured every one of my important careers and helped make a better world—for me and for the people I've touched). I drove a cab for a while, fantasizing that in conversations with my fares, I could help undermine capitalism. But the job was so miserable—12-hour shifts spanning two rush hours in Chicago traffic—that I quickly realized expounding my views with my mostly middle-class passengers hurt my tips, which meant even longer hours behind the wheel. I didn't lie; I just kept my more radical opinions under wraps.

In those days before Uber and Lyft, hundreds of taxis prowled the streets competing against each other all day. Unless you bribed them, the garage men gave the old-timers the good cars, and a bribe was the equivalent of spending an extra miserable hour or two behind the wheel. The cars they gave the non-bribing new drivers had no zip, which you needed badly to beat out other cabs. Once the garage man gave me a cab with brakes that squealed every time I pressed them and back in my own car twelve hours later, I kept clenching my jaw every time I touched my brakes. Some days I'd drive to the garage to pick up my cab, get within a few blocks and then turn around and go home. I wasn't choosing to embrace the rest of the day, but to avoid driving my cab.

I did have one small social revolutionary victory. Two conventioneers from the deep South wanted me to find them some hookers. I started to drive them to a burlesque house way up on the North side where the doorman gave cabbies a few bucks for every fare we brought, but I'd driven only a few blocks when one of them said, "And don't get us no nigger broads, boy."

There was a flop house nearby populated by winos and junkies. I dropped them off and told them, "Go to the desk, say you're conventioneers looking for a room and then just wait in the room for the hookers. It might take an hour or so but they'll be there." I figured they'd either spend hours futilely waiting in a dingy room dodging roaches and rats, or a hooker of one color or another might finally show up, toothless, scabrous, and possibly accompanied by a psychotic pimp. I actually checked the newspapers the next day to see whether any conventioneers had been robbed or killed.

I was proud of that one. Not so proud of the night a guy got in wearing a shabby trench coat, dirty knit hat low on his brow. "Take me to a dirty movie," he said. In my memory, he was actually sniffling into a dirty handkerchief. I suggested *I Am Curious (Yellow)*, a Swedish soft core porn flick. "Seen it," he said. I suggested a porn movie theatre nearby; I had no idea what was playing there, but I knew it would fit his aesthetic. "Been there yesterday," he said. Worried that he was about to start masturbating in my cab, I dropped him off where *Titicutt Follies* was showing, which sounded dirty but was a Frederick Wiseman documentary about an insane asylum in Titticut, Massachusetts.

Even driving a cab, my BA in English Lit came in handy. A downtown movie theatre—those were the days of the grand old movie palaces with the giant dazzling marquees—was showing *I Am Woman*, another Swedish soft core flick, and the theatre had misspelled the star Essy Persson as Easy Person. It was an understandable error but I couldn't let it stand, so I double parked my cab, went up to the box office, and informed the ticket seller of the error. It was the English major in me; I didn't really expect they'd bother changing it. But later I drove past the theatre and they'd actually corrected the marquee. Having participated in anti-war demonstrations, this was the first time I felt I'd had a direct effect on society.

I drove a cab for about three months and then started to regrow my beard, but in 1969, if you can believe it, cabbies had to be clean shaven. They gave me the choice of shaving or quitting. Despite being nervous about how I might pay rent, it was an easy choice.

With no idea what to do next with my life, I felt myself sinking deeper into depression. I had no idea where to go with my life; every option seemed dull, confining, a trap. I decided that I had to sever myself from everything familiar, leave Chicago, the only city in which I had ever lived, and start a new life in New Orleans. Congenitally shy, I decided that if I put myself into a situation where I *had* to talk with strangers, I could cure my shyness, and then things would happen. Sometimes desperation breeds courage.

I knew nothing about New Orleans, except that it seemed like a mecca for the dispossessed and the dreamers. In the days before the safety nets of cell phones and email, I could literally disappear from the radar of everyone in my life and start completely fresh. So with about $50 in my pocket, I boarded the City of New Orleans, heading where I had no place to live, knew no one, had no marketable skill, and no idea what I'd do for money. I imagined New Orleans suffused with a deep blue light, and I hoped I might get a job washing dishes in a Dixieland jazz club.

Around midnight, as the train pulled into Jackson, Mississippi, the naive audacity of my plan began to overwhelm me. I'd be arriving just before dawn with no idea where to go—not even which direction to walk from the station. (This was long before Mapquest; the only guides were city maps in the Yellow Pages in phone booths, and those had usually been torn out). Beyond somehow finding a cheap transient hotel, I had no plans, didn't even know, except for finding the French Quarter (and I had no idea where it was), what to do first and how to put myself among people so that something might happen. Should I grab a few hours' sleep on a bench at the station, killing time until the city woke up? Then what?

A girl my age boarded at Jackson and sat next to me. She had gotten married six months ago and moved to Jackson with her husband. It hadn't worked out with her old man, she said, and she was going back home to New Orleans where her mother was picking her up at the station. I told her my story, and she offered to take me to her mother's house for a shower and a quick nap, and then her mother, who worked downtown, would drive me into the heart of the city and tell me where the nearby skid row hotels and the French Quarter were. "You 'll meet lots of people in the French Quarter," she said. Suddenly I began to hope that my experiment might actually work, that by putting myself into the flow, I might be alright. Riding the City of New Orleans through the Louisiana swamp in the predawn hours, The Big Easy began to realign itself closer to my hopes than my fears.

That morning I found a cheap room in a horrible skid row hotel and balanced my suitcase on top of the small dresser—too high, I hoped, for the palmetto bugs to travel. I'd grown up with cockroaches, but palmetto bugs are roaches on steroids. I started to squash one with my shoe and hesitated, thinking how much gush it would leave, but hesitation is a bad move with a palmetto bug: either let it alone or kill it because when you stand with your upraised shoe, it will stare you down for a second and then, unlike floor-bound roaches, it will launch, sometimes right at you.

I quickly left my room to find the French Quarter, and when I got there I bought an incredibly huge and oily muffaletta sandwich from Central Grocery which I planned to stretch into two meals. Then I wandered toward the levee off Decatur Street, a place of weeds, rats, vagrants and freight cars. (Today it's the manicured and landscaped Moonwalk). I climbed on top of a boxcar and sat, feeling the warm breeze off the river. Sitting on top of a boxcar in New Orleans, watching barges and the Mississippi River flowing easy, hearing the sounds of tugboat horns drifting downriver, I had enough food for the rest of the day, and time completely unfettered from anything I had to do. Even though I worried about how to earn next week's rent, I felt, like thousands of people who have drifted into New Orleans throughout the years, that I'd arrived at the right place in my life.

That evening walking around the Quarter I checked out some bright lights and found they were shooting a Paul Newman movie. They needed extras for a crowd scene tomorrow, and the money would buy me a lot more rent and food. Someone gave me an info sheet about the scene: it took place in the 50's, so the extras would have to get their hair cut short. Thinking about it, I wandered in and out of the soft shadows of the backstreets of the French Quarter, and I wrote in my notebook, "The French Quarter on a spring night is so beautiful it aches." I decided that I couldn't bring myself to cut my hair. I'd have to find some other way to eat.

The next morning I responded to a want ad for able-bodied men to report at 6 AM for day labor to a skid row address near my flophouse. They drove me and a collection of drug addicts, recently released prisoners, and winos to suburban Metairie where we dogtrotted up and down the sidewalks in heat and humidity carrying 15-lb canvas bags filled with 4-page shoppers' newspapers, folding them on the run and flinging them at front doors. The boss man dropped off two men to a block, one for each side of the street, no fraternizing, and as soon as he dropped the last pair, he drove to the far ends of the blocks, picking up the teams one by one and taking them to the next row of streets. When he showed up at the end of your block, he expected you to be waiting for him, and if you weren't, he could decide you weren't putting out enough effort and refuse to pay you. Once in a while he'd drive down your block to make sure you hadn't dumped all the papers in one spot.

Still wearing my Chicago shitkickers, flannel shirt and Levi's, I suffered through the long humid morning. Having already turned down my chance to co-star with Paul Newman, I decided that the entire success of my great experiment in starting over depended upon the

$10 cash they promised at the end of the day. I told myself that I would keep going as long as my block partner, who was in even worse shape than I was, lasted: he'd told me on the van ride to Metairie that he'd recently gotten out of prison, had copped some speed from his old lady's purse that morning to help him make it through the day and discovered, too late, that he'd swallowed her antibiotics instead. Now his guts were cramping up with no bathroom break till lunch. Once, I looked down the block and for some reason the boss man hadn't shown up yet. I turned on a spigot at the side of a house, drank and ran water over my head. (In my memory the water was wonderfully cold, but this was New Orleans, so it had to be lukewarm). For lunch I spent almost $2.00 of my promised ten dollars pay and was still hungry.

My feet blistered, I didn't report back the next day. I had no idea what to do, where to go, so I stopped in at Bonaparte's Retreat on Decatur Street, a bar at a run-down edge of the Quarter. Someone had told me that people my age hung out there, but in the daylight the bar was empty, the bartender bored. I ordered a Dixie beer for thirty-five cents. Eventually the bartender and

I exchanged small talk. He saw I was trying to make the beer last as long as I could, and he handed me a few dollars and asked if I'd run across the street to the French Market fruit and vegetable stand and get tomatoes for the burgers. When I returned, Ed set a free beer on the bar. Later he gave me $20 and asked if I'd run to the bank and bring back rolls of nickels, and that earned me a hamburger and, more important, his trust.

Ed gave me a good tip for lunch. At a shack called Buster Holmes in the Quarter, you could get a big bowl of red beans and rice and a cream soda for $.49 that would fill you up for the rest of the day and evening. Not knowing the streets in the Quarter and too embarrassed to ask anyone, I wandered around and finally found the cafeteria of the D.H. Holmes department store, where I paid $1.50 for a small plate of red beans and rice. (It took me a few weeks before I learned I'd missed the real Buster Holmes). Then I made my way back to Bonaparte's and found a different bartender was working, another bad break Again, I was the only person in the bar. Bonaparte's never came alive until night. He set a Dixie in front of me and I sat there nursing it in the empty bar, waiting for him to initiate a conversation. Fifteen minutes later, I'd taken maybe three small sips when he spoke his first words:

"You ready for another?"

I thought, *the sonofabitch is pushing beers,* and then, almost as if he read my face, he said, "I'm not trying to hustle you. I'm just going to step out for a while in case you want a cold one before I get back."

When he came back, we started talking, and it turned out that he was the manager of Bonaparte's, an empty honorific. It was Friday afternoon, a band was playing that night, and Gordon asked if I wanted to check IDs at the door for something like $1.25 an hour. Within a week I was tending bar there, and Gordon became my best friend until he died about 40 years later.

Tending bar consisted mostly of popping open beer cans and grilling hamburgers on the big charcoal grill behind the bar. There were no beer taps, kegs, or mugs to mess with, and anyone who ordered a mixed drink other than Cuba libre would have been made to feel embarrassed. A few days later I moved upstairs of Bonaparte's into prime real estate, a room where I could stagger to when I got seriously wasted. Even though the six single rooms had no air conditioning or running water and an occasional needle stashed in the common moldy bathroom at the end of the hall, it was a better class of people than at my skid row hotel. Instead of terminal winos and junkies, these were people who hadn't yet bottomed out or permanently damaged themselves, and many never would. It was just the times and our ages.

As bartender at a hangout for winos, offshore oil rig workers on leave, bikers, and longhaired locals and people who'd drifted into New Orleans from all over the country, I found myself one of the central figures in the marginalized community. People told me their stories. I soothed sad and angry drunks and talked people down off of bad acid trips (I had no luck calming meth freaks). When Hurricane Camille was supposed to slam head-on into the city, I sat in a nearby attic with some new friends on a cot that hung by chains from the rafters, and we looked down at deserted Decatur Street, smoking dope, drinking beer and watching crates and boxes and garbage cans fly down the street, laughing that if the roof blew off, we'd still be sitting on the cot, clinging to the chains and flying over the city. Like other hurricanes, Camille drifted east at the last minute, sparing New Orleans a direct hit and going on to devastate Bay St. Louis instead. We heard a radio announcer in Bay St. Louis shout, "God!" and then the radio went dead, further proof that New Orleans and we were charmed. The devastation of Hurricane Katrina was over 30 years away.

Everyone knew that Lala wouldn't live long: he shot up meth several times a week. Lala was about 30 but already looked past 50, toothless and wasted. He would come into Bonaparte's zooming, shirtless and sweaty, literally leaping from tabletop to tabletop dancing insanely. One day he fervently grabbed my arm and looked me straight in the eyes. "Do me a favor," he said. "I really like you. Don't ever shoot up meth. Promise me." I assured him I wouldn't, that I didn't like needles. "Good," he said, "Good. Don't ever start, don't ever start, because—"he began shouting—"If you start you'll never stop. IT'S THE BEST FUCKING FEELING IN THE WORLD!" and off he went leaping across the tables again.

We would give Stan the wino fifty dollars and send him to the bank to get coins. He was that trustworthy. About 40, he always laid the same rap onto middle-aged lady tourists. "Ma'am, I'm not going to lie to you. I need money to buy wine. I'm just a wino. I'm not proud of it, but that's what I am. I didn't used to be a wino. I played football for the University of Alabama. I was really good. I was headed for the pros, and then I blew out my knee." Every word of it was true. One morning Stan died on the sidewalk just down the street from Bonaparte's. Some guys took off his gym shoes, hung them on a parking meter, and the gym shoes stayed there a good week: even the other winos, who scrounged everything, left them hanging on the meter.

Blake and Laura sat at the far end of the bar holding hands. Blake was Black and Laura was White. It happened once in a while within the Quarter, seldom beyond in those days. Two guys sat at the other end of the bar, near the door.

"Look at that nigger, holding hands with a White girl," one of them said, purposely loud enough for Blake and Laura to hear. I went over to them and said, more non-confrontive than I felt, "We don't talk like that in here." I'd gotten half-way back to Blake and Laura when the guy said loudly, "Well, what we got here? A nigger lover. A New York nigger lover."

I was working a double shift and I'd dropped an amphetamine an hour earlier to help me make it to 2 AM, so the racism and code phrase for Jew struck me harder than it ordinarily would have. I slammed my hand on the bar. Sensing they might have gone too far, they walked out while I was already reaching under the bar for a club we kept for emergencies, and by the time I got out the door they were a short way down the block. I ran after them, they heard me coming, turned around and faced me, and at that moment the adrenaline left me and I thought, "Now what am I going to do?" For one quick horrible second we faced each other and then to my amazement they looked terrified, turned back around and ran down the street. I looked stupidly at the club in my hand, as about five people who'd been in Bonaparte's rushed past me, going after them. I watched everyone tear around the corner.

New Orleans seeped inside me. One evening I staggered upstairs to my room above Bonaparte's. I had the room next to Ed, and through his single barred window into the hallway, I saw his cheap curtain had wafted into his room and caught fire on a candle he'd left burning. Ed wasn't there, the fire was spreading, and his door was locked. I ran down the hall banging on people's doors to get them out of there, then ran downstairs and called the fire department. They arrived and put out the fire before it had spread beyond Ed's room. Ed's wall was completely scorched, except for a voodoo mask hanging there, which still shined and glared.

While they repaired his room, we put a mattress on the floor for Ed by the foot of my bed. The next night, sleeping on my stomach, I dreamed a demon was riding on me, its hands on my shoulders, its knees in the small of my back, rocking and rocking, and I *knew* it was trying to get inside me to grab my soul. I tried to shout out to Ed, but it had already gained control of my voice. Terrified, I finally managed to shout out, "Ehhhhhhh!" and I really woke up. But I never felt safe again when I was alone upstairs.

Eventually, I came to feel that New Orleans was *too* easy for me, that if I stayed, I'd continue dropping speed and acid, smoking dope, drinking, and one day discover I was 30, wasted, and still tending bar. I didn't trust myself enough to let my future continue as improvisation in a city so easy. I didn't admit it to myself but I hadn't really purged my middle-class upbringing. So seven months after I'd arrived in New Orleans, I returned to Chicago, my experiment a great success in ways that took me several more years to understand.

On the day I left, old Mrs. Serio told me, "We have a saying here. Once you've been to New Orleans, you'll always come back." I remember hoping she was right. My New Orleans adventure didn't cure my shyness; instead I came to understand that shyness was my learning disability and that although I could compensate for it, I'd never abolish it.

Some days I would stand on the Illinois Central Railroad tracks in Chicago, the end of the line, touch the tracks with my hand, and think, "These rails run all the way down to New Orleans." I sometimes thought, *If I just start walking one railroad tie at a time, eventually I'll get there.* And I did return, many times, for over a dozen Mardi Gras, a lot of Jazz and French Quarter Fests, for Gordon and other friends, and for the city. I hitchhiked, drove, and finally started flying. For years afterward, I'd occasionally dream that I'd arrived back in New Orleans and was wandering down Decatur Street to revisit Bonaparte's. In the dream I was always rushed; I'd marathon-driven the 16 hours but couldn't stay more than a few hours because I had to get back home.

Chapter Six:
On the Road

As an English major, I found a job proofreading and copywriting at Warshawsky's/JC Whitney, the largest mail order automotive parts and accessories company in the country. In those days, almost anyone who ever tried to switch companies, for any reason, was regarded as unstable. You were *supposed* to spend your entire career in one place, so the office consisted of trapped 40-60 year old men whose lives had settled into marriages, kids and mortgages. Although they had to wear ties, they were permitted to roll up their shirt sleeves.

Roy Warshawsky, a mercurial dictator, was impulsively generous but prone to humiliating a person in front of the entire office whenever he was upset. The company was his life, his identity, and he expected everyone else to feel the same about it, but I had immunity from his abuse. I think that Warshawky, who had built a million dollar business out of a west side auto junk yard and didn't care what his employees thought of him, recognized some defiance in me. He also knew that I did an excellent job and that I was willing to quit at a moment's notice, so he had no hold on me. (As added insurance, I schemed to date his daughter, but could never quite pull it off. I was too shy to ask her out and suspected that she was too smart or too afraid of her father to do it anyway).

Bob Zeidman, my immediate boss, was a good man. Warshawsky would often require him and his team to work overtime (with no extra pay) four nights a week for a three or four week stretch, and he'd sit in his office chain smoking and muttering, "Every dog has its day." I was hourly, not salaried, and got overtime for working evenings. Because I didn't have anything much better to do on weeknights and my apartment was depressing, I always stayed to help Bob out. We came to really like each other. About fifteen years later, long after we'd lost touch, he died of lung cancer, and it made me sad.

That apartment. It was the first place I'd lived without a roommate, so I found an affordable illegal basement apartment. To reach it, you had to walk down an alley and then through two dark, dirty gangways until you came to a padlocked wooden door, welcome home. The landlord had tapped into the electric and gas lines, so in addition to cheap rent I didn't pay for utilities. The door opened right into the kitchen which had one barred window practically up against the brick wall of an adjacent building. A narrow hallway with rusted, dirty pipes overhead and a thin frayed carpet led past the kitchen and an old bathroom and ended at the only other room, a small bedroom, which also had barred windows but at least you could look outside and see people's feet on the sidewalk. Dostoevsky's underground man would have killed himself if he'd lived there, but I spiffed the bedroom up with a small bed, a chair from Goodwill, the requisite hippie blue lightbulb which gave almost no illumination and, because every home needs a conversation piece, a giant Styrofoam dinosaur. Warshawsky's—who would have ever thought it?—became my refuge.

My greatest copywriting triumph came during the 1973 gas crisis, when cars lined up for blocks to buy gasoline. Race car drivers had used a vacuum gauge on their cars for years to help determine the best gas pedal pressure for maximum engine power and efficiency, and Warshawsky decided to run a full page promotion marketing a vacuum gauge as a revolutionary new fuel saving device for everyday Americans. By our first monthly meeting after the catalog appeared, the Amazing New OVG gauge had become a top-selling item. Warshawky asked the salesman and manager what OVG stood for, and to their embarrassment they'd never thought to ask me.

"Ordinary Vacuum Gauge," I announced.

Warshawsky scratched his jaw and smiled.

"I'll be damned," he said.

I think he was more pleased about his sales people having to admit they'd never asked me what OVG stood for than he was concerned about the name appearing in a full page spread in his catalog.

The more accustomed I grew to Warshawsky's, the more I felt trapped. Over the next four or five years, I left Warshawky's several times, not counting legitimate vacations, just to escape, and Zeidman always hired me back. My first autumn working at Warshawsky's a friend told me about his hitchhiking trip—all the way to the west coast. Knowing nothing about how to do it, I asked him whether he thought it was feasible for me to hitch to New Orleans that winter.

He said it could be done if I got a very early start

so I could keep heading south as the day warmed up and get far enough south so I wouldn't freeze at night. Hitchhiking seemed like something necessary for me to try, both as a way to keep burnishing my defiant and free Sixties reputation and as a way to keep forcing myself to deal with my shyness. On the road, where no one really knows you, you can be anyone you choose.

I asked Zeidman for a few weeks off. I hadn't yet earned vacation time, but I learned an important lesson about work: do an excellent job and you can usually bend the rules. He told me to call him if I got in trouble. Knowing that I wasn't trapped gave us both some hope.

I took a backpack, a sleeping bag, a map, cardboard and a magic marker for making signs, a can of beans, a can opener, heavy duty mittens, long underwear, a ski mask, and I put on several layers of clothing so that I could keep peeling as I headed south. I rode the 5:45 AM Greyhound bus to Kankakee, 60 miles south of Chicago, so I could start my hitch in safer territory and asked the bus driver to let me off on the entrance ramp of the Interstate.

The sun was just beginning to redden the east, the fields white with snow, the Greyhound's exhaust curling and dissolving into the still winter air, the engine growl giving way to complete silence. Standing at the top of the I-57 ramp, nervous, I saw another hitchhiker way down on the highway, so I stepped past the No Hitchhiking sign and headed toward him, thinking of a verse from *This Land is Your Land:* Woody Guthrie sees a sign at the edge of a field that says, "No Trespassing" and steps past it, over the wire fence and into forbidden territory. The backside of the sign, he sang, "didn't say nothing, this land was made for you and me."

The guy was about my age. I pretended that I knew what I was doing, and we stood on the shoulder of the Interstate small talking. He was going to veer east toward Louisville in a few hours, so we'd be together for just a short time, a secretly reassuring way to start my first hitch. Then a state trooper pulled onto the shoulder, lights flashing, and I learned the script state troopers and hitchhikers followed: they tell you that you can't stand on the highway, you say gosh, you didn't know, that you thought if you stood on the shoulder where the entrance ramp merged it was legal, they play along with your phony excuse and explain no, you have to be up at the *top* of the entrance ramp, beyond that No Hitchhiking sign way up there, and they watch you walk all the way up before they drive off. But you always want to be hitching on the road rather than the entrance ramp; there's a lot more cars to thumb and you're more likely to catch a long ride. So you stand at the top of the ramp until the trooper drives out of sight and then you walk back to the highway hoping you can get a lift before he heads that way again. In almost 15 years of hitchhiking, only one trooper ever doubled back, and luckily I'd decided to go into a truck stop for coffee before I resumed hitching.

At the time I didn't know about the script, and so I was surprised when my new partner headed back down to the highway. I followed him. Once we got to the highway, he went right to the spot where the trooper had pulled over, bent down and picked up a small packet. When he'd seen the trooper pull off the road toward us, he'd palmed his heroin and flipped it under the trooper's car in case he got searched. I was impressed; this was big time stuff.

Soon a car stopped for us. My partner got into the back seat. I tossed my backpack alongside him and sat up front, and when he hopped out at the Louisville turnoff, already learning about the road I watched him carefully to make sure he didn't leave with my backpack.

For the rest of that day and into the evening I made lousy time—short rides, long waits, not knowing whether this was normal or bad luck. (It was bad luck). At one point, just to move and stay warm, I started walking down the highway, thumb out, toward a long hill leading up and over a bridge. A mistake. Halfway up the hill, the shoulder started narrowing, until finally it was little more than the width of my body. Semis rushed past, their wind pushing me toward the edge of the bridge and up against the low guard rail, me fearing that if the driver swerved just a foot, I'd end up smeared on the bridge or flying over it. Semis create a lot of wind when they're rushing past you at seventy miles an hour.

Around eight at night, about 40 miles east of Memphis in flat empty Arkansas country I saw lightning moving toward me. A ghostly cloverleaf junction and bridge were under construction, and so I decided to take shelter there. I found a perfect spot: under the viaduct with a road above to protect me from the rain. Because water would run downhill and collect at the bottom, I walked halfway up the grassy hill, still sheltered by the overhead road, and I laid out my sleeping bag with a thick concrete pillar at my head, so in case it rained hard the water running downhill would part around me. Proud of myself, I crawled into my sleeping bag, popped out my contacts and got ready to eat. Then I discovered my partner had stolen my beans. About a quarter mile down the road the lights of a truck stop promised food and hot coffee, but the thunderstorm had started so the best move was to stay inside my sleeping bag and just try to sleep until the rain stopped.

I woke up soaked. A waterfall running through a crack in the road right above me had drenched my sleeping bag. Shivering from the wet and wind, I tried to put in my contacts, but the wind blew one off my shaking finger into the grass. I couldn't find it so I popped out my other one and dug out my glasses. When the rain finally stopped I wrung out my sleeping bag, tied the sodden lump to my backpack as best I could, and sloshed into the truck stop diner, trying not to look too pitiful and bedraggled—these were *truckers* and I was now wearing *glasses* and everything I owned was miserably wet. I ordered coffee and a sandwich, my shivering subsided, and I nursed the coffee as long as I could. Every time a trucker walked past me to the cash register, not knowing the etiquette, I got up my courage and asked if he was headed to New Orleans.

Finally a trucker said he was headed to Jackson, a good long ride.

"Mind giving me a lift?" I asked.

"You finished with your coffee?" Wise guy. He'd been in there a good half hour and seen me stalling.

"If you're giving me a lift," I said, "I'd be finished even if I hadn't started."

He laughed and motioned with his hand. "Come on along," he said.

As we got close to Jackson we hit another thunderstorm. So much for good luck. "Tell you what," he said, "lemme see what I can arrange for you." He got on his CB, announced he was heading to the 76 truck stop on Gallatin Avenue, had a fella hitchhiking to New Orleans, and did anyone around there want some company.

"Drop him off," said one trucker. "I'm heading on out in fifteen minutes." From being wet, cold and miserable and only half-way to New Orleans, it took me only two rides to get there, one right after the other.

When I got to New Orleans the beans were still on my mind, and after I got settled at Gordon's, I went to a supermarket, bought the exact same brand of beans and ate it for dinner. I kept waking up all night, fiercely thirsty. "Good for the sonofabitch," I thought.

I'd done it, hitchhiked. I spent a week with Gordon, and we did what became a ritual for over a decade on my trips back from New Orleans: Gordon would drive me about 60 miles north of New Orleans to Hammond and drop me off on I-55. I'd be romanticizing it if I said I began my trips back with excitement. It would always take the first good ride to shake off the anxiety and loneliness. And then I would realize that I wasn't doing it only because hitchhiking was all I could afford, but because some experience, good or bad, would rescue me from remembering that off the road my life was less interesting.

Chapter Seven:
More Roads

In a quintessential hitchhiking moment, I'm standing on the highway under a deep blue sky, pure white cumulus clouds drifting along, arcing my thumb in perfect rhythm with the car speeding toward me, my thumb rising as it approaches, reaching the crest of its arc at the precise second the car pulls even with me, then trailing after the car as it passes, not even caring it didn't stop. There's a soft, warm breeze, the smell of freshly plowed spring fields, and occasional drifting *mwahs* from cows who in that very moment also have all the time in the world.

Genuine moments between me and others happened more easily on the road. I hitchhiked for thousands of miles and rides at the perfect time of my life, travelling toward destinations never intended as final. With no obligations to anyone, I kept wandering into good and bad luck. Every time a driver stopped to let me in or let me out, the wheel spun again.

On the road things change quickly, in either direction. One time heading back to Chicago from New

Orleans I was facing a tough series of interchanges through Memphis, and luckily I caught a ride heading all the way through Memphis to the southern tip of Illinois, a good four hour lift though dull, flat Arkansas and Missouri country. He let me off near Cairo at 4 PM, and within just ten minutes another car stopped. The road gods were definitely with me.

"Where you headed?" he asked.

"Chicago."

"Hey, I'm going to Harvey," he said.

A southern suburb of Chicago. The trip was nailed. Less than ten minutes later, we saw a car broken down on the highway and we stopped to help. My driver performed some mysterious rite under the hood, the guy's car started up, and it turned out that *this* guy was going to the north side of Chicago, just a mile from where I lived. I pulled my backpack out of the Harvey car, threw it into the new car, and we started off.

A quarter mile later his car died again, this time for good.

A mother with her two teenage daughters stopped for me. Women seldom picked up hitchhikers, and people with children never did. Ten years ago, she told me, in the middle of nowhere in Alaska her car had broken down, and she'd had no alternative but to hitchhike with her then two little daughters. People were so helpful, so nice, she told me, that she promised she'd always pick up hitchhikers.

A van dealer picks me up, and he's customized it so it's like riding in someone's living room. A great sound system, plush carpeting, and instead of car seats, captain's chairs. There's even a pedestal ashtray between our seats. He offers me a joint and we smoke, listening to the Stones. When he lets me out, I say, "Thanks for having me over," and we laugh.

One time I had to delay a Chicago-New Orleans hitch two days because of a bad cold. Everyone thought I'd headed off again, and so I'd spent the last two days in my miserable basement apartment like a ghost. Meanwhile Chicago's Spring had been doing its usual nasty tease, the winds carrying more cold than warmth. Finally I felt well enough to head out and caught the Greyhound to Kankakee. Six hours later I was in southern Illinois farmland. For the first time in over four months I could actually smell earth, see green. For months, I'd been scrunching up my neck to protect it from the wind, but today I up periscoped my neck into a warm breeze and breathed deeply.

Then the state trooper pulled over, lights flashing.

He wore those badass sunglasses, had a flat stomach, and he walked over like he'd just gotten off his horse. But I smiled at him and said hi.

"You're not allowed on the highway," he said.

"I thought it was legal here," I answered. Feeling too good to keep running through the same old script about entrance ramps and highways, I said, "I've been trapped in Chicago all winter. I haven't seen anything except concrete and dirty snow for months." I waved my hand across the road. "And *cows*. Do you know how long it's been since I've smelled fresh air and dirt, seen animals that aren't on a leash or shitting on a sidewalk?"

I couldn't see his eyes, but his mouth smiled a little.

"You're probably from around here," I said, "so you're used to all this. You're lucky to live out here."

I picked up my backpack and headed toward the top of the ramp.

"There's not much traffic on this ramp," he said. "Hop in. I'll give you a ride a few exits down where there's more traffic."

In Utah, a guy stopped for me and as soon as I got in, he reached under his seat, took out a gun and pointed it at my face. The muzzle looked huge. "Just to let you know," he said, "in case you got a mind to try something." He ended up showing me his hometown: in the middle of miles of rocky, dry land, a gasp of delight, a green, tree-filled oasis nestled alongside a stream. As much as the hidden little jewel of the town interested me, I was struck even more by someone so happy about his home town that he'd made a detour just to show it to me, a feeling about home I'd never felt.

On my way back to Chicago from Boston, I got left off near Toledo on the Ohio Turnpike.

The Turnpike's a difficult hitch. If you try hitching on the actual highway, the state troopers will run you in, no breaks. With so few Turnpike entrances, hitchhikers start stacking up, and the more hitchhikers in one spot, the less likely a driver will stop.

It was a steel gray early winter afternoon, damp, cold, with a persistent wind that snaked through every layer of clothing. I found myself standing there among at least a half dozen hitchhikers.

Four hours later, after two more hitchhikers had

joined us, we worked out an arrangement. We took turns hitching one at a time, the others hanging well back with the understanding that whoever got a ride would ask the driver to fit in as many others as he could. But not one car or truck slowed down to even consider us. My feet were so cold that it seemed my boots didn't have soles on them. Early in the evening, one of the guys sighed heavily, dug into his backpack and pulled out a pair of jeans.

"Anyone got a match?" he asked.

"Burning those won't keep us warm for long," someone said.

"It'll help," someone else muttered.

"We've got to do something," the guy with the jeans said. "It's fucking freezing."

We collected a pathetic little pile of twigs and grass and distributed them around the jeans and contributed our cardboard signs. Someone produced a lighter. We huddled in a tight circle.

"Tie the jeans in knots," someone said. "They'll burn more slowly."

We lit the bottom of one leg and gathered tightly to share some of the warmth. No one spoke a word until the fire burned out. Then the guy sighed again.

"The greatest love of my life embroidered those blue jeans for me in Denver," he said.

"They've been all around the country with me."

They should have given off more warmth. But sometimes love has a long afterlife. About an hour later, a car stopped, and the driver agreed to take one more person. We were unanimous and let the guy who had sacrificed his blue jeans go.

Hitchhiking taught me how narrow my lens had been. I'd been deceived by the anthem of the Sixties in which we endorsed everyone's freedom to do their own thing (as long as they believed in the same basic beliefs that we did). But I met so many people on the road whom I wouldn't have talked with before: salesmen, farmers, factory workers, small-town boosters, Republicans, evangelicals, ex-servicemen, soldiers on leave, truckers, cops and state troopers. I learned that jobs, education and appearances hardly describe a person, and that if I was patient and curious enough to find it every person had an interesting story or a drama. I eventually became a psychotherapist, but through years of hitchhiking I learned more about people and how to connect with them than I did in my psych classes. I tell my counseling students that psychotherapy is like social hitchhiking.

A kid picked me up outside Billings, Montana, a high school senior. Nice guy. He lived in Billings, but he said he'd take me through the city, get me out onto the highway beyond, save me a lot of trouble. Just had to make a stop and drop something off for his girlfriend. They were getting engaged after graduation, and he'd be going to the local college. He lived with his father, and even though his mother lived only about fifty miles away, he hadn't talked to her in years.

"When I was two, my dad went off to Nam, left my mom alone with me. The whole time he was gone, she didn't feed me nothing but cokes, pizza, fast food. My bones didn't grow right." He looked normal enough, but when we got to his girlfriend's and he stepped out of the car, he tottered on his spindly and crooked legs so badly that every step he took, I worried he'd pitch forward.

"Need some help?" I asked.

"Naw, I use a stick when I go hiking in the mountains, but this here's nothing," he said. "Thanks anyway." His girlfriend was beautiful, open and sweet. You knew just looking at her, she was the pick of the class. They both had easy laughs.

Back in the car, he talked about his upcoming graduation. He already had a part time job lined up in land management while he studied forestry at college. I asked if he was going to invite his mother to his graduation.

"No," he said. "I understand why she did it. She was angry at my dad for going off and leaving her. But it don't feel good to see her."

When he left me off, he wished me luck and told me to be careful.

In Mississippi, an ex-sheriff's deputy picked me up. He'd recently been fired, he said, for political reasons.

"What kind of political reasons?" I asked.

"I burned a cross on a nigra's lawn."

I couldn't sympathize about him burning a cross, but I knew he was right about the political reason. Just in the last year or so the Feds had finally started prosecuting racist sheriffs. A year earlier the sheriff would have been at his side burning the cross. My silence made me feel complicit in his racism, but it felt too dangerous to challenge him. We were in the area where about ten years earlier Cheney, Schwerner and Goodman, a Black and two northern White Freedom Riders, had been murdered by local Klansmen.

After a while, he asked me, "Why do you hitchhike?"

"Sometimes it's been hard for me to talk with people," I told him. "Hitchhiking puts me where I have to do it."

I wasn't sure how that laid with him, and we drove in silence for a while. But often when you confide in people, they feel safer about confiding back. He told me losing his job was only part of how bad his life was going. A few weeks ago his wife found out he'd screwed his next-door neighbor. He'd only done it once, but she'd found out and kicked him out of their house.

Here was something a little less dangerous we could talk about. I said, "Man, I don't know how it is for you, but I've been finding out that when I fuck someone just for fucking, as soon as it's over, I feel bad and just want to get out of there."

There was a long, uncomfortable pause. First I'd told him I was shy and then that meaningless sex didn't feel good for me. A Northern liberal, maybe even one of those homosexuals.

"I know what you're saying," he said. "Me and my wife are starting to see one of those marriage counselors next week." He said he'd thought he hadn't loved his wife anymore, realized he was stupid, and hoped this marriage counselor would help them put things back together. Now that he'd gotten fired, he was scared she'd leave him for sure.

On my first trip hitchhiking to Seattle, everything went wrong. It was close to 10 PM, I was making lousy time and still in Minnesota, thirsty with an empty canteen and nowhere to get water or food. The exit ramp said Worthington, but I couldn't see anything down the country road. The next Worthington ramp was two miles ahead, and that one would have motels and restaurants for sure, but two miles seemed a long walk with such awful thirst. A sign said there was a regional airport down this exit, and I could just make out its lights in the distance, so I decided to head down the country road, figuring I'd go into the airport terminal, find a snack bar and get something to drink, maybe even sack out a few hours on some seats if they didn't kick me out.

About a half mile down, terribly thirsty, I knelt and ran my hand lightly across the grass. The dew was heavy, so I took off my bandana, rubbed and rolled it around in the grass and chewed the bandana. Not enough moisture to make any difference.

The airport, a further way down and then a good distance off the road, turned out to be completely locked up for the night. I walked back to the country road and continued walking and walking, musing about passing out from thirst in the state of a thousand lakes. Sooner or later there had to be a small motel or a diner. Eventually—too late to do any good—I realized that I should have stayed on the Interstate and just walked to the next Worthington exit. Finally, long past midnight, after walking miles, I found a motel. The restaurant was closed, so I just bought some vending machine candy bars and orange juice, and chewed ice in bed until I fell asleep.

I knew I should get an early start the next morning, but when I thought about walking back along that long road to the Interstate I decided to go into the motel restaurant for breakfast instead. After breakfast, I asked the cashier if there was a shorter route to the Interstate. She looked at me strangely.

"The Interstate's right over there," she said.

I had walked for hours on a curving road that brought me the long way to the next Worthington exit.

After breakfast the road picked up. I caught a ride clear out of Minnesota and into South Dakota. I had never seen country like South Dakota. Treeless hillocks of yellow grassland, stretching from one horizon to the other, rolling like the sea. The Great Plains. I stood on the side of the highway under a deep blue cloudless sky, hearing the wind whiffle through the grass. I decided to step off the highway and walk to where there was nothing but me, the sun, the sky, the wind, and the grass. Five minutes later, I stood behind a little knoll that blocked the highway sounds. Standing alone, I breathed deeply.

Suddenly, a huge shadow raced across the land and swept over me and I froze in terror. Then I realized the shadow was just a solitary cloud passing across the sun. I shook my head, amused, and understood how much we lose growing up in a city where there's so many shadows we don't even think about what each one belongs to.

When I walked back to the highway to continue

hitching, a state trooper pulled alongside me. "Sorry to bother you," he said. "I just need to check your ID. We're looking for an escaped prisoner." He checked my ID, wished me good hitching, got back in his car and drove off.

I'd made it to the West.

If the good times made me feel more alive than I'd felt in years, so did the bad.

Hitchhiking taught me that sometimes we have no power over what happens, but that sometimes we do. Deep in Louisiana swampland, I could feel lonely and scared, listening to the croaking and chirping in the night or I could play my harmonica to the moon. If a ride suddenly seemed dangerous, I might be able to do something to ease the situation but nothing would save me for sure.

As we drove down a rural highway, I realized the guy who'd just picked me up was seriously drunk. When he talked to me, he fixed on my face and the car would drift toward the other lane. Once to redirect his eyes to the highway, I pointed to the windshield crack right in front of his face. "When'd *that* happen?" I asked.

"Jest last month," he said, and he opened his mouth to show me some missing teeth.

He started to tell me about his time in Nam, his voice growing louder. "You know what they did to us over there!" he suddenly shouted, and he clamped his huge hand on the inside of my thigh. Anxiety amplifies my shyness, but sometimes terror overrides it. I had no choice. I had to get on top of his mood, so I grabbed his hand, pried it firmly off my thigh and stared hard into his eyes.

"I don't like being touched," I said, sounding ice crazy. He mumbled, "Sorry."

He let me off at the next exit ramp. Night had fallen, and I decided to walk a little way down the road, then go into the woods and sleep a while. That way if he came back looking for me, he'd assume I caught a ride and was long gone. I found a soft spot under some pines, unrolled my sleeping bag, stripped down to my underwear, and climbed in.

Then I heard a branch snap. Someone was walking in the woods. I told myself to stay absolutely still. I didn't see any flashlight, and if I didn't make a sound he couldn't find me. I lay still, listening hard, breathing as shallowly as I could. Then I heard another branch snap, closer. I'd looked down the road when I'd left it to make sure he'd really driven away. But if he'd been spying on me, he wouldn't have let himself be seen. *He was in Nam,* I told myself. *He knows tracking.*

I eased out of my sleeping bag and soundlessly slipped into my pants and shoes. I crouched, knife in one hand, flashlight in the other. If the next branch snap or footstep was close, I'd flick on the flashlight and shine it straight at him, temporarily blinding him so I'd have an extra few steps head start and run out onto the highway, hoping a car would be coming along. Then I heard a footstep just a few yards away; I wheeled and flicked on the flashlight, catching a goat in its beam. I'd been sleeping near a fenced-in pasture. It actually *mahhhed* at me.

In Nebraska, around 2 AM the biker picked me up. Bikers usually don't stop; their bikes are already loaded with gear with no room for your backpack. "Hey, thanks for stopping," I said.

"But where we gonna put my pack?"

"Keep it on," he said.

He wore a black cutoff shirt, with biceps as thick as my thighs. Headband and sunglasses, even though it was nearly midnight. A chrome sissy bar with a serpent gleamed in the moonlight.

I didn't think I wanted this ride, but there wasn't much traffic, and you don't refuse an offer from someone who looks like he would eat you for breakfast. So I squeezed between him and the sissy bar. In order to fit, I had to raise my backpack high, so that half of it was above my shoulders. I put my arms around him loosely.

"You ready?" he shouted over the engine.

Like his ride offer, it wasn't a question you could say no to. He kicked it into gear and we roared onto the highway.

The wind slammed so hard into my pack that I worried I might go flying backwards over the sissy bar. I clutched him tighter. Despite the cool night, he was sweaty. I glanced at the speedometer. We were doing ninety. The backpack straps pulled at my shoulders. I thought maybe I could shift forward a bit and lower my pack, but at ninety miles an hour on a bike you want to be still. Make that ninety-five, closing in on a hundred.

Then a semi-comforting thought came to me. It was

good that we were doing a hundred.

I'd be just as dead if we lost control at 60, and at a hundred we'd get to our destination more quickly. I leaned forward and shouted into his ear, "Where you headed?"

"North Platte!" he shouted.

At a hundred miles an hour, we'd be at my turnoff in just two hours. A terrified dialog ran through my head.

"Two hours are lots of seconds. All it takes is one second to die."

"We're doing a hundred. That means less seconds."

I leaned forward and shouted again.

"What're you doing in North Platte?"

"Gonna rob a bank!" he shouted.

At least that changed the dialog inside my head.

"He's just fucking with me"

"He's crazy, he's going to rob a bank!"

Then a third line of dialog joined the chorus.

"He's cranked up on amphetamines!"

I couldn't think how to respond. Finally I shouted, "Good luck!"

"Won't need luck!" he shouted back.

About ten minutes later, I decided to talk with him

some more. It's dangerous to engage a crazy person in conversation, but I didn't feel comfortable leaving him wandering around with his own thoughts.

"Making great time!" I shouted.

This time he delayed before answering. "Man!" he finally shouted. "Good thing you said something! I was falling asleep!"

"Glad to help!" I shouted back, silently discarding my amphetamine hypothesis.

A few minutes later, he pulled off at a roadside diner. "Need some coffee," he mumbled. I thought about staying outside and trying to catch another ride, but I didn't want to offend him. It was a sleepy diner, with only a few people inside silently sipping their coffee and picking at their pie. Our entrance reminded me of a badass desperado kicking open the swinging saloon doors. "HOW YOU ALL DOING?" he shouted. One person barely looked up from his coffee, and the others ignored him.

"WE HAVIN' FUN TONIGHT?"

That got him a few nods, which seemed to satisfy him. He downed three cups of coffee in about ten minutes, and stood. I insisted on paying, thinking about the old

European custom of tipping the executioner so he'd do a clean job lopping off your head. Then I followed him out to the bike.

"We got some time to make up," he told me as I squeezed behind him.

About forty-five minutes later, he pulled into a rest area. "Gotta get some sleep," he said.

I saw my chance to escape. "I'm not sleepy," I told him. "Gonna try my luck some more."

"Well, if you're still out there when I start up, just hop back on."

"Thanks," I said.

Past midnight in western Montana, on an empty mountain highway, I thought about finding a place to sack out for a while. The road was slow, down to one truck or car every ten minutes. I could see each one miles of downhill road away, small headlights in the vast night. Well, at least the circumstances favored catching a truck, which meant a long ride. There was a truck lane just ahead, so they'd be slowing down on the steep grade, making it easier and safer for them to stop. A beat-up Chevy slowed down to check me out, then kept going. Disappointed, I stared at its taillights and was surprised to see its brake lights suddenly flare. It pulled off the road some distance away, and I grabbed my pack and trotted uphill to the car. Two guys were in front, and so I climbed into the back. When I settled in, I asked them where they were headed. "Down a ways," the driver said.

At best that meant a short ride. At worst, vague answers about destinations sometimes meant trouble, and they were drunk and getting drunker. A long miners' strike had just ended, they told me, and they were going back to work tomorrow. Not the kind of situation in which I would have gotten blind drunk and stayed up all night, but if the job is miserable enough....

"You get high?" the driver asked.

"When I can get it," I replied. I wanted to make it clear that I wasn't carrying any dope; I didn't want them to think I had anything worth taking. "It's too expensive for me these days," I added.

"We got some weed here," the driver said. Then they pulled off at the next exit ramp, turned onto a dirt road, and drove about a half mile into a dark and deserted field. No one had ever bothered to pull off the road to smoke dope; usually we just smoked as we drove along.

Then they shut the engine and the silence and darkness thickened. I slipped my knife out of my belt sheath, silently opened it and held it in my lap. If I hadn't been so scared, it would have been the loneliest moment of my life.

"We don't have papers," the driver said.

"Me neither," I said.

"We could make a pipe with this can if we had a knife," his friend said. "You got a knife on you?"

Had they seen the hunting knife on my belt loop when I'd gotten in?

"Nope," I lied.

Strength and adrenaline determine who wins a fight. I knew I didn't have the strength; it was two against one, both of them much stronger, and *my* adrenaline fuels terror, not aggression. I told myself I'd have to slash right at the throat of whoever reached back first, then quickly slash at the other guy. *Fast, don't hesitate, there won't be a second chance.* I tried to prime myself but kept doubting whether I could really do it, the kind of thinking, I knew, that guaranteed I'd lose. What if they didn't really mean any harm, if they'd turned around just to talk with me and now I'm a murderer?

What if they both turned? Slash wherever the cutting edge is facing.

"Well, hell," the driver said. "I guess we can't smoke." He started the car and we drove back to the highway. The moment they reached the highway, they stopped, and I got out safely. Why had they picked me up in the first place? Were they hoping I had papers? Did they just pick me up on a drunken whim? Had they intended to rob or kill me but seen the knife when I got in? Had I just been paranoid? And had they really just driven off or were they planning a sneak attack?

The moon was behind the mountains. Standing on the road, I studied the highway shoulder.

Loose rock and gravel, so I'd hear them if they tried to sneak up on me. Far below, a pair of headlights slowly climbed the steep grade, and I heard the growl of a semitruck. *Please pick me up*, I thought. *Please.* A driver in his safe cocoon, driving through the vacuum of the night, he'd probably just drive on past, listening to his radio or thinking about love, loneliness, daily chores and plans.

Please pick me up, I thought. *Please.*

He did, and even better, he was going to Fargo, North

Dakota, the longest ride I had ever caught. Safely inside the truck, I was leaving the mountains far behind, heading back into the Great Plains.

Around the middle of the day, I realized that my shoulder blades had been getting sore for some time. Trucks bounce on every bump and small dip in the road, which is why drivers' seats are spring mounted. After hundreds of bounces, the skin on my shoulder blades was scraped raw. Just after twilight, he pulled into a truck stop on the outskirts of Fargo. I could barely slip my backpack onto my sore shoulders. I said so long to him and walked to the highway, and then I decided to get some sleep before I began hitching. Exhausted and sore, I needed to give my shoulders some healing time. I walked into a grassy field. The grass was nearly thigh high, and I walked far into the field to get away from the headlights on the highway, the truck stop lights and the highway noise, tossed my pack down, unrolled my sleeping bag and fell asleep on my stomach. Just before I nodded off, I thought about lying on my back and looking up into the stars, but my shoulder blades were too sore.

I woke in the false dawn, walked back to the

highway, stuck out my thumb, and within five minutes I had a lift, a local guy going to the other side of Fargo.

"Don't think I've ever seen country this flat," I said. "And I'm from Illinois."

"We can see an anthill ten miles away," he replied. "In the winter, we get three feet of snow and by the next day the Canada winds have blown it all into South Dakota."

I told him about my good night's sleep in the field. He looked concerned.

"We never go in that field," he said. "It's full of rattlers."

I hoped there wasn't a surprise coiled inside my backpack.

My hitchhiking days are almost 50 years in the past, and sometimes still when I drive past the downtown Chicago exit ramp on the Kennedy expressway, I remember getting out of someone's car at 3 AM, having travelled all the way from New Orleans, walking up the long sloping grassy embankment that thousands of people drive past daily without ever imagining that anyone ever walked there. I remember stepping over the curb that separates highway territory from the city and into silent, sleeping downtown Chicago wearing my backpack and walking over to the el to re-enter normal life, temporarily glad to be back home, but already starting to feel depressed.

Chapter Eight:
Riding the Rails

The first time I rode a freight train was on another hitching trip from Chicago to New Orleans. The hitching had gone terribly slow; it was early evening, and I should have been well beyond Memphis, but I was still only in southern Illinois. Worse, a heavy fog had rolled in, so thick that drivers couldn't see me until they were whizzing past. Most drivers don't stop out of enthusiasm but instead on a hesitant whim: they like to check you over before they decide, and in the fog they couldn't see me until the last minute when it would be too dangerous for them to pull over. Far downhill, maybe a half mile away, I heard a train horn and could just make out a freight train stopping. Desperate, I thought: maybe, maybe and started walking through knee deep wet grass. But the train pulled out well before I could get to it. I was both disappointed and relieved.

But I was holding the dice in my hands, and there was no sense going back to the highway. I went into the small station—it was little more than a shack—and not knowing what else to do I played the innocent pathetic card, telling the railroad man I was trying to get to New Orleans for my godson's baptism—a complete lie. Midway between adventure and capitulation, I asked when the next passenger train was due, thinking that if the timing was right I'd just walk several miles to the passenger station in Cairo and buy a ticket. Not until late tomorrow afternoon, he said. Only half acting, I looked disappointed. "Why don't you just hop a freight?" he asked. "There's one coming through in about an hour."

A railroad guy suggesting I hop a freight was counterintuitive, surprising.

"How do I know where it's going?" I asked, thinking, *I'm going to do this!*

"I guarantee you it's going to Memphis," he said. That's where they all go from here."

I thanked him and walked a good quarter mile down the tracks so when the train stopped, I'd have already checked out a lot of boxcars for an open one. I found a piece of cardboard, laid it down in the tall damp weeds, and lay on my back, looking up into the night fog, awed at what I was about to do. *Hopping a freight.* Finally, I dimly heard its horn, then saw its headlights in the distance glowing through the fog.

By the time the first quarter of the train had rolled past me and then stopped, I'd seen no open boxcars, so I held my backpack against my chest and began trotting toward the rear. The train started up. I finally saw an open car coming toward me but I was surprised at how quickly the train picked up speed and that the boxcar floor was chest high, a tough leap. Making a reckless decision I tossed my backpack inside. Now I had no choice but to get on. I slammed my hands onto the boxcar floor and took a few running steps, the train's speed giving me just enough momentum to make the jump. I think I made it only because I was panicked about losing my backpack. (Years later I learned that you should never leap onto a moving train. If you misstep, you get sucked underneath the train and, if you're lucky, you only lose your legs.)

As soon as we passed the shack, I stood in the open doorway, pulled an imaginary train whistle cord and actually yelled *wooo wooooo!* Twice. I stood looking out at the foggy swampland, awed at what I'd actually done, and then finally went into a corner to sit down and relax. About a 2 ½ hour drive from where I was to Memphis, I figured the freight train would take about that long.

I hadn't known that freight trains make so many stops. It took hours to reach Memphis, and by then it was afternoon. Not wanting to end up in the freight yard where I might get arrested for trespassing, I stood in the open doorway searching for the highway to orient myself so I could look for a place to hop off without finding myself disoriented in a dangerous neighborhood. But at ground level in cities, freight trains don't go through safe neighborhoods. A few people saw me and waved, and I felt admired, even envied. *I'm the guy riding the freight train!* Finally I spotted the elevated highway about a mile off in the distance, but now we were going through downtown Memphis, high fences on both sides of the tracks, and before I knew it we were in the freight yard, in trespassing territory. Nothing to do now but wait until the train finally stopped. Then I climbed down and started walking down a long row between two trains, hoping to find a way out before I got spotted, trying to be quiet in the silent trainyard, my footsteps crunching on the gravel. Then a railroad guard stepped into my row. Just to let him know I only wanted to leave the train yard I waved and asked him where the highway was, even though I could see it in the distance.

"Where you headed?" he asked, and I told him New Orleans.

"There's a train building up on track 7 headed for Vicksburg," he said. "It's leaving at 5:45."

A few hours from now, one ride 250 miles, then a straight easy shot from Vicksburg to New Orleans, and I wouldn't have to hitch through the nightmare of Jackson, which could take hours just to go ten miles. I'd be practically home free. On the other hand, it was three o'clock in the afternoon, I hadn't slept or eaten anything for over a day and a half, I was thirsty, and freight trains don't have dining cars. Still, I'd be in Vicksburg in a few hours where I could easily find a truck stop by the highway. I walked over to track #7, found an open boxcar, climbed in and made myself comfortable—*this* was the way to hop a freight. At 6:30—almost an hour later than scheduled—we lurched off for Vicksburg.

It ended up taking me close to 18 hours to get to Vicksburg, after a night of hallucinations. I'd gone too long without sleep or food and not enough water, and my electrolytes slipped way out of balance. Sitting against a back wall of the boxcar, I saw a woman in a long flowing robe standing at the open door, slowly waving a long sword back and forth. I told myself that it was just a piece of baling wire tacked above the door frame and blowing in the wind, and I knew this was true, but I also knew that the apparition might be true as well. Reality, I reminded myself, is merely a widely agreed upon construct, and when you're exhausted enough you might actually be seeing a different reality that's always been there. *This is what all crazy people tell themselves,* I attempted to reassure me, and I answered, *This is how all deluded sane people dismiss the reality that's actually there.*

I thought I should walk to the open door to determine the truth and then realized that *this* was insanity. She might behead me and, even if it were just a hallucination, what if I slipped more deeply into it and leaped in terror from the boxcar highballing through the Mississippi countryside, killing myself? Because I couldn't trust what was real, sanity dictated cowering in a back corner of the boxcar, holding my knife open and keeping close watch. As soon as we got to Vicksburg, I leaped off the train, walked to the highway, ate a quick breakfast and stuck out my thumb, and the next ride went all the way into downtown New Orleans, less than a mile from Gordon's apartment. I was so late arriving that he'd begun thinking I'd been killed on the road. Riding the freight trains, I'd been untethered from everyone, freed from every social obligation, a sometimes terrifying freedom.

CHAPTER NINE:
INTO THE MOUNTAINS

Hitchhiking helped me feel less shy and bulked up my adventurous reputation, but it didn't hit another sweet spot: being alone without feeling lonely, which is an alluring refuge for a shy person. That sweet spot is possible only when there's no *possibility* of human connection—no telephones, doorbells and random encounters. So over a period of about 7 years I went on lone backpacking trips into the Rockies, to the Raweh Wilderness in northern Colorado, where I wouldn't see or hear anyone for several days. Some moments in the Raweh were difficult and some frightening, but it introduced me to a peace and an awesome beauty and solitude I never could have known in the Midwest. It was also, though I didn't realize it, a way to both escape my father's Boy Scout ghost and to travel with it.

One day I lay for several hours in a high mountain pasture, reading, meditating, napping, then reading, meditating and napping some more. Above timberline in the late summer months, you live in synchrony with the clouds: the sun warms you until a cloud glides across it, the temperature dips, and you slip on a light jacket until the cloud passes, and then you fold your jacket, lay it down in the grass and make a pillow out of it. I spent an entire afternoon gazing at distant mountain peaks or at a few wildflowers next to me. Suddenly I heard a couple of thumps. Sound travels far in the thin air, and I thought, "Goddamn it, somebody else is in the area putting up a tent. There goes the solitude." Then I saw two deer about forty yards away standing still, watching me. I had no idea how long they'd been standing there, but the male had finally decided to announce his presence by thumping his leg. I kept still and pretended to ignore him while he kept cautiously coming closer, stepping and pausing, stepping and pausing. Almost an hour later, he was finally so close that I could have touched him, heard him breathing, saw scratch marks on his side from his days of brushing against trees and walking through bramble. I understood that because I'd been so relaxed, I had become part of his world. He hadn't come to welcome me—that idea belonged to my ego—but to explore me, to just be next to me. I felt I was in a state of grace. By now it was dusk, getting chilly. I sat a while longer watching him walk around my campsite, and I finally whispered good night to him and went into my tent. Late in the night, I heard him still hanging around, and from the sound of footsteps, I knew his mate had joined him. In the morning they'd gone, and the handle on my mess kit skillet was bent where one of them had stepped on it. The mess kit never again fit together snugly because of the bent handle, but I kept using it.

Photographs seldom evoke visceral, sensory memories for me. But the photographs in my mind…. Wood's scarce above timberline, so during my daytime hikes away from my tent I've gathered twigs. I've found small rocks to build a compact fire ring so a random gust of wind won't carry off a spark and start a grass fire. (With all the improvements in backpacking stoves and with climate change's hotter, drier mountain weather, building fires in wilderness areas is now prohibited). It's late dusk, time to start my fire. I've gathered dry pine needles for kindling, and I build a little teepee of twigs over the pine needles. I learned this way back in Cub Scouts, in Illinois and southern Wisconsin state parks, where the object was to build bonfires that obliterated the darkness while we shouted and laughed to overpower the noises of the night, told ghost stories and roasted marshmallows. Now I'm sitting on a rock slowly feeding twigs into my campfire, which is more glow than flame, listening to its hiss and crackle. Then my internal camera switches spots, and I'm several yards away watching my barely illuminated back and wondering what the man sitting by the small campfire is thinking. I smile at the vestige of ego and come back into myself sitting on the rock looking at the fire. Staring at the shadowed mountain peaks and the stars splashed across the sky. Listening to the faint rushing sound of water and a breath of wind from far away that I know will arrive in a few minutes to drift across my campsite and then move on. *I'm here*, I think. *Here.*

Once at the urging of friends I took a satellite phone. I never used it, but just knowing it was in my backpack diluted the trip. By bringing the possibility of connection, it imported loneliness.

Occasionally in my solitude I did end up glad to connect with someone. The trails in the Raweh are fairly well defined, but one day I was in too much of a hurry. It was mid-morning of my last day, and I had a five hour hike to get out of the wilderness and to the highway to begin my hitchhike back to Chicago. Somehow I lost the trail and got off onto a game trail. By the time I realized it, I was still above timberline instead of down in the forest, and a thunderstorm moved in. You don't want to be above timberline in lightning where you're the tallest object. Plus, I knew that my poncho wouldn't completely cover my mountain backpack and gear in the rain and wind. I found a thick branch, held it straight up and down for support, and squatted for close to 45 minutes during the storm so the poncho would keep everything on my back covered while thunder and lightning crashed around me, worrying that if the lightning didn't kill me, the storm would wash out the game trail so I wouldn't be able to backtrack. My thighs ached from the squatting, then started spasming, and my nerves were fried.

When the storm finally passed, exhausted, I managed to pick up the game trail again and backtracked to the actual trail. Just as I reached it, a couple of horsemen rode past and looked at me. "Man," one of them said, "looks like you could use this." He handed me down a small flask. I took one swig of the peppermint schnapps and it bloomed so fully inside my head that they saw its effect, and we all started laughing. "Looks like you need one more," he said. Then I checked my topo map with them just to make sure I was headed in the right direction and I started off. But I'd lost too much time; I'd never make it out of the wilderness before dark. I pushed a while longer but by dusk I still hadn't made it below timberline, and I had to choose an iffy spot to pitch my tent: too out in the open, between two treeless grassy hills, so if it rained the water would rush down at me from both sides. But it was safer than camping on top of a treeless hill in lightning and more comfortable than sleeping in the mosquito-infested forest a half mile further downhill.

At about one in the morning, a big storm hit, and my tent floor started getting wet. It's bad wilderness policy to tear up the ground, but if I didn't dig a gutter around my tent, I was going to get flooded. Even though I didn't want to get out of my tent, I had no choice. Frantic, lightning flashing and thunder crashing around me, I trenched strategic spots around the tent, muttering and whimpering during the lightning and thunder. I sat straight up all night in the middle of my sleeping pad, my backpack and gear crammed on the pad around me in case the trenches didn't work.

The storm finally stopped at dawn. When my tent and groundcloth were dry enough to pack up, I started out again. Around noon, I finally got out of the Raweh, made it to the road, and stuck out my thumb. It was about 25 miles of slow road to the Interstate just outside of Fort Collins, so it took a while. As we neared the Interstate, it started to rain *again*. My ride was going past my turnoff at the Interstate and I was exhausted from the tension, the thunderstorm on the game trail, and the long sleepless night. I decided that I'd had more than enough goddamn rain and needed the certainty and comfort of a bath and a bed. It was close to 6 PM, so I checked into a motel near the on ramp. I sat in a warm bath for close to an hour, washed the woodsmoke from my hair, and decided that I had just enough energy to eat and walked into the motel steakhouse.

Several times in my life, this fantasy had occurred to me, but it had never materialized until now. The waitress was my age, and we both felt the possibility in that cozy steak house by the Interstate where transience was baked into the atmosphere. Completely uncharacteristically, I suggested we get together when she was done working. She said sure, she'd be off at 10. Even more uncharacteristically, I wrote down my room number on a napkin and gave it to her, so she'd come to my room. Then I told her I was going to grab some sleep—I'd already regaled her with my stories of the dangerous thunderstorms—and she should come by when she was off work. I bought a small flask of whiskey and went back to my room and crashed.

Deep in sleep I heard a soft knock on my door, so soft I wasn't even sure I'd heard it. I looked at the clock. It was 10:15. The soft knock came again. I knew that we would have to do drinking and talking, and I felt too exhausted to last through any social preliminaries, so I put the pillow over my head and immediately went back to sleep.

All I had to do was answer that knock on the door and enter into an ideal fantasy. I would have predicted that the next day and even for years after, I'd have regretted not doing it. But instead I'm still satisfyingly bemused. The gift you want so much sometimes obscures the real gift. I'd had an adventure of fear and improvisation, and discovered what I could do when I had to do it, and what I didn't need to do just because I could.

PART THREE:
LOVE AND LOSS

Is It Really Better to Have Loved and Lost?

A cliché is something that's been so true for so long that it's come to sound meaningless. Take "It's better to have loved and lost than never to have loved at all." But after a breakup, if you can get to the place where you genuinely believe it—not an easy or short journey, and one we'd seldom choose – digesting a lost love becomes more than just a consolation prize. It actually becomes a pendant or a charm bracelet to wear for years instead of just a trophy that gathers dust sitting on your shelf or stashed in a closet. When love itself turns out to have been only a temporary wonderful cure, and you eventually realize it had more value than the pain of its loss, you've done well in the mortality race.

CHAPTER TEN:
THE VAMPIRE UNDER THE VIADUCT

I lived for years with fear and an occasional actual attack. From the time I was a kid living with my father's anxious warnings about anti-Semites growing more numerous daily or our family heading for the poor house, anxiety has tinctured my life. Until about the age of seven, every night when I got into bed, the second I switched off the lamp on my nightstand I had to immediately get my arm and head under the covers because something was going to kill me in the dark. I'd leave a small breathing space by my nose, making sure not even an inch of it stuck outside the blanket. Oddly enough, most people see me as a risk-taker, a romantic, an adventurer. Give me enough time to tell my stories about hitchhiking, riding freight trains and going on solitary backpacking trips into the mountains and I'll mention how anxious I often was when I started a trip, but some people think I'm seasoning my adventures with false modesty. Everyone needs heroes.

Though I'd never have chosen anxiety to be so much a part of my make-up, I'm somewhat grateful for it: it's motivated me, fueled adventures. When I realize I have a choice between giving in to my fear or taking action, I usually act because it would feel worse living with myself knowing I'd surrendered to it. I often tell my psychotherapy clients who pause and tremble on the brink of change that bravery doesn't mean the absence of fear. Bravery means acting *while* you're afraid. People who act without fear are usually fools, not heroes. So I suppose by my own definition, you could call me brave, as long as we understand that the braver I am, the more frightened I'm feeling.

One night in my late teens I found myself literally surrounded by about ten gang members, with their leader intent on badly beating me. He stepped into the center, faced me, and told me to throw the first punch. I was not a fighter, and I knew that even if I was lucky enough to knock him out with the first punch—hardly a possibility—the rest of the gang would still close in on me. Besides, I didn't have it in me to hit someone unless I was actually in the middle of fighting, and maybe not even then.

"I'm not going to fight," I said, trying to radiate calm certainty instead of whining fear.

Confrontations like this, when one person intends to fight, follow a familiar escalating script. "What's the matter? You afraid?" he sneered.

"I'm just not gonna fight," I said, having no option but to play out the script and delay getting seriously hurt for as long as I could.

"Fucking chickenshit Jew," he said, upping the ante.

"I'm not fighting," I repeated.

The next step called for him to shove both hands against my shoulders, but to my surprise he skipped that one. I never even saw the punch. Instead, a cymbal clashed inside my head and my cheek erupted. I fell a step back from the impact; why it didn't knock me down remains a mystery. What I do know is that my head and thinking immediately cleared. I knew that the punch wouldn't end things, that no matter how I responded, it was just a prelude to a severe beating. I had only one chance. I reached into my pocket and took out my brass knuckles. A year ago I'd gotten jumped and ever since then I'd carried them in my pocket. They were a security blanket, not a weapon; I always knew that I wasn't capable of using them. But I also knew, in my adrenaline-charged clarity, that my only chance now lie in carrying out the best bluff of my life. I crouched in a street fighter pose—something I'd seen in movies like *Rebel Without a Cause* and *West Side Story*—stared him right in the eyes, and said calmly, "OK, motherfucker, come on."

He smiled hard, and I saw that my bluff wasn't working. He liked this game. I had just given him carte blanche to do even more violence. But I could only remain crouched and sneering, playing out my hopeless hand to the end. "Wait there," he told me, and he went back into the restaurant they'd just left to get his jacket, which undoubtedly had *his* pair of knuckles. Surrounded by his friends, I watched him walk into the restaurant as though I were eager for him to come out so we could finish things up. My attitude relaxed his friends enough so that when I broke at top speed through their circle and disappeared around the corner, no one even made a grab for me. A sprinter on our track team, I knew how to run for my life.

In high school, I was one of the fastest sprinters on our team, but my most vivid memory is crouching on the starting blocks, waiting with terrible anticipation for the starting gun, knowing each start could be the one I'd blow. I never knew the feeling of confident anticipation waiting for the starting gun.

As I grew older, my fears faded but never vanished. One night when I was in my twenties, I got pleasantly stoned and went for a post-midnight walk in the park. The park was deserted and silent except for the crickets. I was underneath a very long viaduct, near the halfway point, when I suddenly felt that a vampire would silently come around the edge of the viaduct ahead of me and step onto the path and that if I looked back, I'd see another one already standing behind me, so that I would be hopelessly trapped by their cunning and supernatural powers. The thought lasted only a second. Then the fear of vampires turned into one of muggers. It had been years since I'd read about the three Billy Goats Gruff, but the troll under the bridge still waited for me.

Several times, what looked like my bravery was an even greater fear of looking like a coward. On a logjammed Chicago street, some guy decided that if he squeezed into the small lane between the parked cars and the line of cars moving inch by inch he could gain a few car lengths and then squeeze back in, delaying everyone else even more. When he tried to get in ahead of me, I wouldn't let him in. He knew I was deliberately not yielding an inch, thwarting his agenda and challenging his manhood. Mostly I just wanted to impart a small lesson about how people in societies ought to behave. Eventually he crept forward a few more car lengths, where someone more obliging let him in. Then he got stopped at a red light, and here he comes, stomping toward me, raging and waving his arms. The social script called for me to roll up my window, lock my door and sit there while he humiliated me by yelling and banging on my car roof. The scared part of me wanted to do exactly that, but I was even more hesitant to look like an intimidated middle-aged guy in front of strangers. So when he got to my car door, I looked up at him calmly—*much* more calmly than I felt—and reasonably said, "Well, just because you wanted to get in didn't mean I had to *let* you in." He immediately stopped shouting while his brutish brain tried to process a set of rules he hadn't thought of. Then he turned around, started raging again and walked back to his car.

Fear often haunted my desire for love. Allowing

myself to love, or to feel loved, inevitably raised the specter of rejection. Only the love I found in fatherhood didn't frighten me. Even during Alex's adolescent years when she shouted once or twice that she wished I'd die, I knew she said it only because she knew, unlike at least one of my ex-lovers, that her wishes didn't have the power to make it happen.

From adolescence on, my trajectory with love ran the same course as my other adventures: for some time after a breakup it took a while to reach the point when the accumulating negative consequences of playing it safe would begin to feel worse than the fear of trying, and then I was ready to try dating again. It's a tribute to the power and glory of love that when it finally comes, it washes away lingering traces of fear for a while. Maybe having lived with fear makes love even *better* when it arrives, like the news as soon as you come out of the anesthesia that things look good and you're safe. Love becomes like the moment when the enemy has passed and the sound of their footsteps grows dimmer until you can barely hear them. Then you take a deep breath, scramble up the embankment, loudly inhale and exhale, and notice how vivid the colors, smells, and sounds of the world are. One day love happens to spot fear sitting far off in the distance on a lonely hilltop and laughs, thinking about the old Laurel and Hardy film in which Stanley's still patrolling a deserted Pacific atoll years after the war's ended.

CHAPTER ELEVEN:
WANDERING PARTNERS

In my third year at Warshawsky's (with several hitching and backpacking breaks) I finally had my first live-in girlfriend. A divorced co-worker at Warshawsky's was having an affair with a married woman who lived way out in the boonies. Because Jeigh lived with his adolescent daughter, he couldn't bring Diane to his Chicago apartment, so my basement hole was perfect for their assignations. One Friday night she had no way to get into Chicago so she had her friend Cheryl drive her in, promising her a double date with a real city guy. Born and raised in Antioch, 50 miles from Chicago, Cheryl had wanted to escape for years to the city and start living. Always the gracious host, I let Jeigh and his woman take the bed, and Cheryl and I took the floor mattress. Under the watchful eye of the Styrofoam dinosaur and the dim blue lightbulb, orgasm after orgasm reverberated in the bedroom.

When you're lonely and in your early 20's, sex quickly metamorphizes into love. Cheryl's romantic image of me bulked up my ego and my love for her.

She found in me an opportunity to escape from her marriage to a provincial lout and live in the city with someone who knew what city life was all about. Cheryl liked how I preferred to walk through alleys rather than down sidewalks. In alleys, I explained to her, you could see what the city was really like behind the facades. She affectionately called me Ghetto Rat.

Just a month after our first meeting she left her husband and moved into my pad with her Siamese cat and Irish setter. There's something to be said about the insubstantial life: major changes are easy to make. I hadn't learned that there's often a pattern to how someone leaves their relationships, and it took me two years to wonder, when our own relationship finally crashed, whether her husband had actually been such a bad guy.

My bed was so small that we had to sleep hugging each other, which was fine, except that the cat, who disliked being cold, insisted on staying in bed too. When we fucked, the cat rode on my back and as Cheryl and I got more excited and the cat's ride grew rougher, it would dig its claws deeper into my back. Then when Cheryl started moaning and screaming, the dog would start growling at me.

Within a few months the glory of living in a city rathole wore off, and Warshawky's had started to wear on me again. Cheryl had introduced me to a certain level of comfort she'd imported from the country, things like fluffy blankets, towels that were actually thick enough to absorb moisture, dishes with floral designs, and spoons that didn't bend when you dug out ice cream. The idea of me going to grad school in a small town offered an escape from a life that was starting to feel confined, a way to kick the can down the road in terms of our already fading love and our lack of any idea what to do with our lives. Once again, I left Warshawsky's. As part of my anti-identity politics I didn't want to live like a university grad student, so instead of living in the university town of Carbondale, Illinois, we found a place in the next town over.

Many people don't realize that southern Illinois is south of the Mason-Dixon line. With the Vietnam war tearing the country apart, the Murphysboro people didn't like long-haired students. So although I avoided grad school life as much as possible, when we walked down Murphysboro's Main Street drivers occasionally wolf whistled or tossed beer cans at us.

Shortly before midterms, the National Guard killed and wounded thirteen students at Kent State, and several hundred Southern Illinois University students staged a sit-in in downtown Carbondale, blocking the Illinois Central railroad tracks. The state troopers—Southern Illinoisans not kindly disposed to liberals and students—warned students on loudspeakers to clear the tracks. There was a long, silent standoff. Everyone knew what was coming next. When the tear gas canisters landed, the crowd ran into downtown Carbondale, and I yelled, "Carbondale dies!" The ensuing riot couldn't be attributed to my yell though I'd like to think it played some small part. Just to make sure, as everyone ran toward mayhem my second shout actually got taken up by some students: "No midterms!"

A few hours later, when tear gas and billyclubs had reduced the student hoarde to isolated knots of stragglers, I avenged the Kent State shootings. A trooper was amusing himself by driving up and down the street lobbing tear gas at small groups of exhausted, defeated students who were no longer rioting, and so I stepped off the curb, flung a brick and smashed his windshield. It wasn't just Kent State propelling the brick: things weren't going well with Cheryl and me. My savage joy of flinging the brick quickly dissipated when I realized that if the trooper stopped his car and came after me no one would save me, so I ran, figuring Cheryl would follow, and if she didn't, she'd be okay because he'd be chasing *me*. We found each other later that evening and never talked about it. We were so inept at relationships that talking would have only made things worse.

Trying to find a life that would work better for both of us, I left grad school and we returned to Chicago, where I went back again to Warshawsky's while Cheryl found a secretarial job. Our new plan was to save enough money so we could go hitchhiking around Europe for as long as our money lasted. We found a cheap apartment on the north side of Chicago, the only slum building in a decent neighborhood—a nine story building with about ten one-and-a-half room units on each side of a dirty linoleum-tiled hallway and a cage elevator that worked most of the time. (Fortunately there was a backup freight elevator if you didn't mind riding with stinking garbage cans). It was a hot, humid day when we went to check the place out, and Nick the janitor/manager wore a long sleeve sweater.

"Lemme make sure the apartment's OK," said Nick, and when he went into the bathroom and ran his fingers under the wash basin, I knew the sweater covered his track marks and he used empty apartments to store his needles and dope.

The unit was so small that it had room for only a small musty couch, a table and two chairs, a tiny sink, a two-burner stove and a murphy bed. The two windows offered no cross ventilation, which meant that if we wanted to breathe at night we had to keep the door to the common hall open, not a safe thing in that building, so before going to bed, we'd build a tower of cardboard boxes in the open doorway. That way thieves would wake us if they moved the boxes.

Adam and Marie, a 40-something year old couple, lived in the unit next to us. Adam was under five feet and easily weighed 275, and Marie had bleached blonde hair, thick tinted glasses, and a voice graveled from spending years perched in neighborhood bars. At four in the afternoon they'd start drinking, and by six o'clock they were cranked up and screaming at each other. "I *love* you," Marie screamed at him once, "and if you don't believe it, then *FUCK YOU!*" I actually got out of bed to write that one down. Another woman at the other end of the hall seemed to get along just as poorly with her partner. Every night she screamed torrents of profane abuse. One day I said to Nick, "That woman down the hall really doesn't get along with her old man."

"She lives alone," Nick told me.

We couldn't get to Europe soon enough. In 1972, long before the Common Market, Europe was inundated with so many hitchhiking, panhandling, long-haired young people from around the world that the border guards stopped letting people in who looked like us unless you could show them you had enough money. In the era before credit cards, everyone travelled with traveler's checks, so on our second or third week in Europe, we walked into the *polizeistation* in Hamburg, a cold stone fortress that would have terrified my grandparents' families, and we filed a police report, falsely claiming that our checks had been stolen. (We needed an official report to get replacement checks from American Express). Although we couldn't use our original traveler's checks—that would have been a serious felony—after our replacement checks ran low, we kept showing the old checks to the border guards to "prove" we had money on us. When we couldn't find a hostel we snapped our two Army ponchos together to make a crude pup tent and slept in fields. About two or three times a week we'd get a cheap hotel room so we could clean up and get a good night's sleep.

In a half year hitchhiking from England through France, Belgium, Germany, on up to Denmark, Sweden and Norway, back down through Austria, Yugoslavia and into Greece, we were part of a great movement of people like us, living cheaply and unencumbered by thoughts of the future as long as we kept on the move finding new experiences. We ignored the fact that the future is always coming at you whether you move in a straight line or keep zig zagging.

The glorious youth vanguard was not as homogeneous as we thought. In Amsterdam we stood in line to get into a cheap youth hostel. Because the capacity was limited, we got there two hours early to join the ragtag line. We were hungry though, and I suggested we leave our backpacks in line and go get something to eat. With some difficulty, Cheryl persuaded me that it wasn't such a good idea to leave our backpacks unguarded, so I brought back food while she stayed behind. Finally we got into the hostel, tossed our packs onto our bunkbed and read notes on the bulletin board like, "The motherfucker who stole my camera, I hope you die." The shower room was co-ed, about twenty showerheads in a row, with no stalls or even half walls in between. Cheryl wanted to pass on showering, but I told her that if she stood under the showerhead and faced the wall she wouldn't know anyone was looking at her. Her decision to do it might not sound like a stretch today, but I wouldn't have been impressed by my grandfather's liberation story about the first time he walked out of his apartment without a hat or tie, or my great grandmother recalling the first time she stepped outside without wearing her bloomers (or wearing them; I'm not sure what they were).

Late one afternoon near the beginning of our long hitch from Salzburg, Austria to Thessaloniki, Greece we just couldn't catch a ride for several hours, so we finally resorted to the old hitchhiker trick: I hung back in the trees and Cheryl stood on the road alone. Within ten minutes a driver stopped, and I emerged and climbed into the back seat with her. It was already dark when we hit Yugoslavia, and our driver began driving erratically, swerving. Looking at his face in his in his rear view mirror I figured out why: he kept staring intently at Cheryl.

After a while he said, "Tired, sleep now," and pulled onto a deserted dark country side road. There was silence in the car, silence outside, and I decided I had better stay awake. Suddenly the car was flooded with light and a car blared its horn; our dazed, mysterious driver had parked right in the middle of the deserted road. He drove on a little while until he came to a hut, went inside, talked to the old lady who lived there, then told us, "Come."

We were on the outskirts of a small village. It was close to midnight, and we were tired and had no idea how to get back to the highway, so we had no choice but to go inside. The entire hut consisted of a kitchen with a wood-burning oven built into a wall, its back protruding into a small bedroom with a dresser and a bed that took up most of the room. That was the entire hut. No bathroom, just an outhouse and a small sink with a pump. The three of us had to share the bed. (I had no idea where the old lady would sleep, but he had obviously worked out some deal with her and paid her something). Cheryl and I slept with our clothes on, holding each other, and he laid across the foot of the bed. Every so often when a car drove by and its headlights brushed across the bedroom, we saw him propped up on one elbow staring at us, just staring, all night long. We took turns elbowing each other when one of us fell asleep.

In the morning, the old lady appeared and cooked breakfast. Eggs fresh from the hen and milk direct from the cow. Then we were on the road again heading for Greece, with a full day's driving ahead just to get through the rest of Yugoslavia. He'd said he would take us all the way into Greece, but at five o'clock at night, near Kosovo, only about ¾ of the way through Yugoslavia, he announced he was tired.

"We go hotel," he said. "I pay. I buy you dinner."

The thought of a shower, good bed and a free meal was tempting. We told him that was fine but we had to have our own room, and he agreed. We got into our room, showered, changed clothes and met him in the restaurant. I ordered chateaubriand; I wasn't sure exactly what chateaubriand was but I knew it was some kind of high-class steak, and I figured he owed it to us after the last night, a 26 year-old's sense of entitlement. The chateaubriand turned out to be stringy swiss steak with peas slathered on top. Before dessert came, I went to the restaurant washroom, and I learned later that while I was gone he'd leaned over to Cheryl and said, "Come my room tonight."

"I can't," she said. (When she told me the story, I silently took offense that she'd said "can't" instead of "won't").

"No think," he said. "Come."

She didn't. In the morning we went to meet him in the lobby at the prearranged time but he had already checked out and left. We were glad to lose the ride until the desk clerk informed us that he hadn't paid for our room or the dinner.

Later that day we reached Thessaloniki. It was about five years after the fascist Colonels had staged their coup and overthrown the democratic government, and I realized for the first time how the shadow of fascism darkens everything. We were driving through the city having a friendly conversation with our driver about his life, his city and Greece, and then I asked him whether things had changed since the Colonels had taken over.

Up to then, he'd been garrulous. Now he stopped talking and looked around before he answered, even though it was just the three of us in his car. "It is more difficult now," he said, and went silent. I changed the topic and mentioned how beautiful Thessaloniki was. I learned how Fascism doesn't exist just in the superstructure of society; it seeps into everyone's bones.

Eventually we returned to the US, and I returned yet again to Warshawky's. This time we found a decent apartment, but after close to seven months in Europe, our relationship, with nowhere else to go, continued deteriorating. It took close to a year before we decided to try a trial separation. I hitchhiked to New Orleans to live for a month with Gordon, hoping—I hated melodramatic flicks, not realizing that I often lived one—that if we spent a month apart from each other things would heal. But we had long passed the point where we needed each other's physical presence to keep fueling our resentment. A month later she wrote and said we had broken up. Because our lease still had six months to go, I wrote back that I'd stay in New Orleans for a while and she could just keep deducting my half of the rent from our bank account. After five months I decided to finally hitchhike back home so we could figure out the bummer logistics about splitting possessions and deciding who'd live where once the lease ended. I phoned and asked her to send me $30 from our bank account so I could have some money in my pocket for the hitch home.

"The bank account's gone," she said, in a dead calm voice.

"What do you mean gone?" I asked.

"A guy in a bar said he had an investment. I gave him our money, and he disappeared." She didn't even try to make it convincing. $752 was a lot of money in those days, all I had. I hung up on her and told Gordon that there was no sense going back home, that I'd stay in New Orleans for good. "If you don't go back and let her steal everything," he said, "you'll regret it for the rest of your life." Gordon bought me a plane ticket, so instead of hitching I showed up unannounced at our apartment two days earlier than she'd expected and discovered that she and her new lover had packed up everything except what reeked of me—they'd tossed all that stuff into an alley dumpster weeks ago—and they were planning to move out the next morning so I'd come home to an empty apartment.

CHAPTER TWELVE:
ARBEIT MACHT FREI

It took me a while to climb out of that one. When I pulled the surprise raid on the apartment and they left in a furious huff—how dare I show up unannounced like that?—I changed the locks on the doors and quickly sold Cheryl's baby grand piano. Then I went to the neighborhood health food store and asked the owner if I could get some groceries and I'd pay her back in two weeks. It was like when I hitchhiked: although I had enough money from selling the piano, I needed to re-enter humanity by putting myself into a situation where I was dependent on someone's good will.

It was a cold, drizzling spring, and there were occasional stray cats in my neighborhood so I carried dry cat food with me. One day I heard a small kitten mewling under the bushes in front of my apartment building. I offered him some food, and he followed me home. In case he wanted to find his way back to wherever he'd come from, I kept my back door open. He left that night but returned in the morning, and for the next 16 years, in almost a half dozen apartments and houses, he spent most of his life outside, an amazing life span for an outdoor Chicago cat. I named him Sunrise partly because of his yellow gold color and partly because I felt he marked a turning point for me, a way to help me feel a little better about my life. I had no idea why my relationships didn't work out; I just knew it had something to do with me. Sunrise and I trusted each other completely.

Meanwhile, a new secretary got hired for our department at Warshawsky's. Terry and I soon worked a way to stretch our half hour lunches into an hour, She'd punch out and leave for lunch at 11:30, and at noon I'd punch her timecard back in, punch myself out and go for my own lunch. She'd return at 12:30 and punch me back in. Everyone knew what we were doing, but we always got our work done on time and did excellent jobs, so no one cared. But one day, Bob Zeidman's boss, unhappily married, propositioned Terry, and she turned him down. In those days no one ever filed sexual harassment suits—there weren't even any protection laws on the books—but after being rejected he was uncomfortable around her, and he fired us both for the time cards. Zeidman had tears in his eyes. I felt bad for him but also relieved to have found a way out of my self-imposed Warshawsky trap, and I filed for unemployment compensation.

I collected unemployment comp checks for six months, and Sunrise and I moved in with a former English professor of mine who had a large house. (More on Mary and me later). But despite having enough income from the checks and few expenses, I had no direction and no love. To help me find my way back into life I developed the Exercise. I spent afternoons sitting on a shopping street perched on a storefront window ledge about waist high with all the passersby, forcing myself to meet people's eyes and smile as they approached. I tried to convince myself I was conducting a sociological experiment—how do people react when a stranger smiles at them?—but I really hoped that smiling at people would help me poke out of my shell and land a miracle connection. (These were still the days before the Internet and online dating sites). The best I got were occasional smiles, random sparks. Usually without any eye contact people would quickly look into the area beyond my head. The worst were the blank stares right into my smile, as bad as a rejection. One mother with two children walking toward me, all three in a line holding hands, switched places with her kids to put herself between me and them. Immediately contemptuous of her fright, I quickly devolved into feeling like a leper.

A friend told me her friend Sheldon was working for a small company and looking to hire a driver. I called Sheldon and we arranged to meet at a bar. The job sounded good. DHL, recently starting out, had no logo, no company uniforms, no rules or requirements for drivers other than to pick up and deliver documents to businesses, ship them out from the airport, and avoid car accidents. The salary was good, I got to keep the car 24/7, DHL paid for the gas, and I got car and health insurance. Sheldon hired me immediately. I met all the requirements; I knew how to drive and I was Bev's friend, and so a few hours later we staggered outside. The next day I met Sheldon at the DHL office, which was his living room. We drove the car to a neighborhood gas station and filled up two large trash containers with garbage that had been accumulating in the car for months.

I never saw DHL as a career. I kept two pens in my shirt pocket, one for customers to sign for their packages and one for my own writing during down times between stops. I never polluted my writing pen with DHL work, and I never dignified my DHL pen by using it for personal writing. One time I delivered an envelope to a top executive at Amoco Oil. His south penthouse office windows overlooked the city and his east window bank overlooked Lake Michigan. He wore a suit that cost more than I'd spent on all my clothes in years. He looked at me and shook his head ruefully. "When I was your age," he said, reaching for his fountain pen to sign for the documents, "I had to decide whether to be a forest ranger or come work for Amoco. Every fucking day of my life, I've wondered whether I made the right decision." It wasn't often I felt my career choices validated. I told him he couldn't use his fountain pen because the receipt had a carbon, and I handed him my DHL pen.

Eventually, Sheldon quit to go to law school, and DHL began to get more corporate. I stayed and DHL grew quickly; soon the Chicago office had about 20 employees, a real office, personnel policies, a standardized company fleet, uniforms and a company logo. When I'd started, DHL had a one-person Human

Resources department in Honolulu that focused on treating employees well rather than on protecting the company, but now the department had metastasized into protecting the company and snipping benefits while explaining to workers why all the changes were actually for the workers' benefit. For a while they tried to adapt the Japanese management style—company and employees as mutually loyal teammates—but they quickly switched to the UPS management style of strict monitoring of productivity and pressure to work harder. They adopted a pay raise scale based solely on performance statistics and supervisors were told to fire the bottom lowest performers each year. Then the next year's raise scale required even higher levels of performance. Hamsters on a wheel.

I managed to insulate myself from DHL's tightening noose by going part time as their Weekend Supervisor While the weekday operation was closely monitored, the station manager and operations manager couldn't compare our weekend productivity statistics to the weekday's: during the week, there were morning delivery crews and afternoon pickup crews, and an airport operations crew, but because most of our client companies worked only a half day on Saturdays and tended to call in unscheduled last minute pickups, Weekend Ops mixed everything together. I took advantage of our unique position and stayed overstaffed.

I made sure my weekend ops people understood that if they did their jobs well, we could avoid scrutiny. But one day the Station Manager announced he would come in on Saturday and work the dispatch radio so he could monitor our routes in real time. This was trouble. Fortunately about ten companies would call up on Friday afternoons to schedule Saturday pickups, and I snuck into the office on Friday night and pulled most of the orders. Then on Saturday morning I alerted our secretary that she'd be getting phone calls from me pretending to be customers with pickup orders, and when I called them in she should run them into our Station Manager who would be working dispatch monitoring the routes. When he laid out the routes he saw clearly that Weekend Ops was overstaffed. But after a driver would drop off his packages, say, in a northern suburb and had driven halfway into Chicago I'd go into another room and call my secretary with a pickup order for the suburb he'd left 20 minutes ago. When legitimate pickup requests came in, our drivers, on the day's new tight routes, couldn't get to them before their offices closed. As all of the supposedly tight routes began crisscrossing and doubling back on themselves, pickups and deliveries began running late and angry customers started phoning and asking where the hell our drivers were. Our manager got so frazzled that he left early. I followed him to his car, patiently explaining once again why weekend routes just couldn't be planned and run like the weekday ones.

What I'd learned at Warshawsky's once again came in valuable: do an excellent job and you avoid close scrutiny. It's just that DHL's definition of excellent performance differed from mine: I believed in delivering good service and treating my employees well, while too many companies define excellence as continually rising profits. My crew's statistics were excellent (it's easy when you're overstaffed), our customers lauded our service, and I saved DHL some money by figuring out creative ways to save money on shipping, though the balance sheet was still tilted toward keeping my employees happy. I stressed loyalty to my crew—not loyalty to DHL, but to me and to each other.

Once, when one of our courier's routes got too busy,

I asked Don, who had the route next to his, if he could handle two more stops: I suspected that during his route Don had been stopping at a health club and getting in a workout—the gym bag in his car was a good clue—so I had my lead tail him and secretly snap a photo of him coming out of the club. Then next Saturday I asked Don to take on the two extra stops.

"I'm really maxed out myself," he told me.

That was a violation of the spirit I tried to cultivate. My weekend ops people helped each other out, partners in larceny.

"Maybe you could cut your workout a little shorter," I said, handing him the photo.

Don got the message. No punishment, no lecture, and don't lie to the person who's on your side.

DHL gave my life no meaning or pleasure, but thanks to my health insurance, I finally started seeing a therapist and eventually decided to go to graduate school—two simultaneous grad schools in fact, one for Social Work and one for Creative Writing. Therapy may have helped me finally find a direction, but for a while I hoped it had not unleashed something worse, and that too much of a direction could get in the way of living.

CHAPTER THIRTEEN:
THE BOTTOM OF THE LEVEE

I married Sandy when I was 39. I'd never dated—in fact I'd disdained—someone with a life like hers: she worked hard at sales, made lots of money, owned an expensively furnished home, and unlike me based much of her identity upon her job. But I'd just come out of therapy and for the first time in my life I was ready to venture into unknown territory with someone who embraced middle-class values. More surprisingly, although I hadn't thought seriously about having a child, within three years we were married and had a baby.

No one, myself included, would have expected me to ever become a father. But Sandy and I wouldn't have stayed married if she'd been the only one of us who wanted a child; I'd previously thought of children as part of middle-class quicksand. Maybe the shift had something to do with biological imperative; males have biological clocks too, and now I was past 40. Also, Sandy and I were in love, and raising a child seemed a good part of it. Maybe, too, it was partly the desire to redeem and rework my own upbringing, to do right what hadn't been done right for me. Unlike my father, I vowed, I would pay close attention to my child's learning and discovery for *her* sake more than for my ego. And unlike my mother, I would pay attention to my child's feelings and support them; she could feel whatever she wanted to feel, and I'd be there with her, even when she'd get angry at me or wouldn't go along with my agenda.

Never having been one to set personal goals, this was a pretty lofty agenda. One day when Alex was in third grade I was walking her home from school and she got mad at me, nearly nailing me with her book bag and decimating a bush with it instead.

"You're really mad," I said.

"You're a psychotherapist and that's all you can say?!" she shouted.

I marveled how with just one sentence she could make me feel like a failure as a therapist *and* a father. But instead of feeling too bad, I thought that someday great things might be in store for her.

But first there was the firestorm of her baby colic. Months of her screaming and crying every waking hour. She was inconsolable; nothing soothed her except movement—she stopped screaming only when she was being rocked, hugged, taken for walks in her stroller, or riding in a car. The minute the car stopped, she'd start in again, so I'd drive ten miles an hour down streets, timing the stoplights two blocks ahead so I wouldn't get stuck at a red, oblivious to impatient drivers who honked at me or gave me a finger as they shot past; their anger was nothing compared to Alex's screaming. "There's nothing we can do for colic," our pediatrician said. "We can only treat the parents. Take shifts with her and when it's not your shift get out of the house."

Human beings are hard wired to respond to babies' screams; it's helped our species survive. But when you can't soothe your baby or stop the screams, your internal alarm bells start jangling, and that can lead to trouble. In the suburb next to us, a father was arrested for deliberately swinging his baby into a wall, and for the first time in my life I understood how thin the line is between compassion and desperation and between love and violence.

Sandy was working long hours at her high pressure job during the week and I had a very small psychotherapy practice in our house. We found a retired nurse who kept our colicky baby in her home for several hours a day so I could see a few—very few—therapy clients to supplement my weekend supervisor job at DHL. On weekends, Sandy was the sole caretaker and Alex's colic was as brutal on her as it was on me. She began to resent working hard all week and spending her weekends alone without any husband around to help.

As New Orleanians learned years later, people aren't aware that the underwater base of a levee has been gradually eroding until the levee suddenly collapses. The excitement, joys, distractions and hard work of raising a child hid the cracks that had been present in our marriage for some time. In the next few years after Alex's colic became just a memory, aside from being a father, the sense that my life wasn't working right slowly returned. I got paid so well for working two days a week with full-time benefits that I never built up my therapy practice and had no idea how to do that anyway. But it got increasingly difficult dodging corporate incursions and bullets while working at a job that meant nothing to me. I had become my middle-class father.

As Sandy and I slowly became aware that the differences between us weren't the cause for celebration we'd originally thought, the differences started fueling resentment. It's a common pattern in a souring marriage: you're attracted to the missing parts of yourself that you find in the other person, but eventually when you can't integrate those parts inside yourself, you begin to resent the other person for having those same traits. Sandy had been attracted by my defiance, my unconventionality, my determination to be creative and to avoid the kinds of traps that society lays for us. I was attracted to Sandy's determination to set a goal and go for it full tilt, to make money and to have the world reward her for her accomplishments. Eventually, though, I saw her as compulsive and she saw me as an irresponsible failure.

Our differences continued seeping into the widening cracks. Our different attitudes toward defiance and socially approved behavior played out in raising Alex. I would sit her high chair at my right side during dinner, hold a spoonful of spinach to my mouth and say, "My favorite food, spinach, I'm sure looking forward to eating this." My attention would wander off to my left, my spoon would drift toward her mouth, she'd eat the spinach off my spoon, and then I'd come back to attention and discover my spinach had mysteriously disappeared. I'd look disappointed and puzzled, and we'd go through the game again. After the third time, I'd begin to look at her suspiciously and she'd put this innocent look on her face. She was not only getting away with eating my spinach but she was adding dissembling to her defiance. I liked that.

When she was old enough to walk, we'd go to the park, and I'd be a giant who liked to eat little girls. The first time I did this, she looked scared, but I began to cry. After all, that's what giants were supposed to do, and now my mommy and daddy giant would be mad at me for not eating her, and all my other giant friends would make fun of me too. She started lecturing me that eating little girls was wrong. Then she started distracting me by offering imaginary pieces of broccoli, which the giant couldn't resist. I stressed subterfuge and defiance over accommodation and obedience, a good strategy in measured doses for raising a child but not so effective in an adult love relationship.

When Alex was about five years old, Sandy posted a chart on the refrigerator so Alex could earn gold stars for things like good behavior, bringing dishes to the sink, and other tasks and responsibilities. "I'm not going to raise our daughter like a behavior Nazi," I said, which, I'll admit, may have been an overstatement.

As Sandy and I each retreated into our familiar patterns, our disappointment in each other deepened. Sandy worked harder, and I decided to go once again on a solitary backpacking trip. It had been several years since I'd backpacked. I had something to prove, to myself and to Alex and Sandy. That's when I almost died.

CHAPTER FOURTEEN:
THE CAVE OF WONDERS

During her fifth year, a few months before I got lost in the Pecos, Alex fluttered her hands by her ears and sang in a taunting, sing-song voice, "Fitcher's got a big butt, Fitcher's got a big butt," and I had no idea where she'd learned this or who Fitcher was. I realized that those days had gone forever when I could figure out where every idea and word in her mind came from. Her learning had expanded well beyond my teaching and surveillance.

One day she put the cover from the wok on her head and said she was someone from *Mortal Kombat*, the year's most violent video game. Even as I admired her creativity, I wondered which one of her relatives on her mother's side had introduced her to the game.

Horses and art became her two biggest interests. The first time she rode a horse, she sat way up high with a calm smile on her face. She developed an interest in everything equestrian and quickly acquired several toy horses—a big gray one called Magic, a smaller pink version named Beauty, and two even smaller plastic ones, Shiny (or sometimes White Beauty) and Beecephalus. She refused to believe me that the proper name was Bucephalus, which, incidentally, was the name of the horse of her namesake, Alexander the Great, one of those coincidences which can seem to imply that time, space, and all of us exist on a quilt bound together by invisible stitching. She also acquired a zebra named Laura, and zebras, as everyone knows, are really horses in pajamas. As far as art is concerned, her figure drawings suggested an aptitude for metaphor and a suggestion that Buddhism might someday prove a useful tonic: the grasping arms came directly from the head. By June, the arms had gravitated down to more or less where they're supposed to be, midway between the head and heart.

On the darker side of art, she became interested in death, and that knowledge would now give more depth and shadow to her hopes, plans and adventures. Things without shadows are one-dimensional. If you don't want death around, try enjoying a bouquet of plastic roses. (The mom of a high school buddy of mine, a highly anxious woman, used to protect her plastic flowers from dust by encasing them in plastic). Some of Alex's earliest questions about death: When I die, will I be able to hear? Is Grandpa Herb dead forever? Dad, are we going to die at the same time? Grandma, are you going to die soon? (This to Sandy's mother the *second* after Dorothy blew out the candles on her 60th birthday cake).

There are different kinds of death in this world. Less than a year after I returned from the Pecos, Sandy and I finally decided to divorce. Only Alex had been holding us together, which was too much of a burden for her to carry. We couldn't teach Alex about love and intimacy just by talking it up, and we couldn't fake it. She began picking up on something sour in the air. "How come you never sleep in mom's bed?" she asked me. One day as Sandy walked past, Alex looked at me and asked, "Why are you looking mad, Dad?" During the awful year and a half divorce proceedings, one night Sandy was crying in bed while she and I talked about divorce, and suddenly we realized Alex was listening outside the door. What she heard and, more important, what she made of it we would never know, but we invited her into the bedroom and when she asked why mom was crying, we said mom had just had a nightmare. Three days later she mentioned her mother's nightmare again. Alex began having more frequent nightmares herself.

How can you explain a divorce to a child? Any agreed upon truth that parents tell their children about their divorce ends up camouflaged in clouds of euphemism. Although we never overtly fought in front of Alex, the household tension was palpable. Sandy told her that we were divorcing because even though we loved each other, we couldn't live together. I suppose on some level that was true, but our love for each other had become an historical artifact, and I don't think it reassured Alex.

No matter what Sandy and I finally worked out, Alex was going to go through the three biggest transitions of her life. She'd move from the only home she'd known into an apartment, not a house, in a different suburb. Her mom and dad would be living apart from each other, and she would begin at a big kids' school where she didn't know any neighborhood kids. One day during the long divorce battle, I looked at Alex playing on the floor with her horses. The day before, Sandy and I had taken her to see *Aladdin*. Today I wanted to tell her to imagine the world before her as a huge face, like the Cave of Wonders in the movie. The mouth in the giant face opens wide, its tongue rolls out onto the sands and stops at your feet, beckoning you to step onto it and walk into the gaping mouth. Would she be scared? Excited? Curious? Sad? Ready to go? Sometimes we choose our adventures, but sometimes they choose us. The worst response to a potential adventure, even worse than fear, is boredom, but this is one of those lessons she wouldn't learn for decades.

Under the custody agreement, Alex lived with me weekdays from Mondays after school until Friday afternoons when Sandy would pick her up, keep her all weekend and drop her off at school Monday morning. To help acclimate Alex to our new place, I got her a bunk bed so she could sleep snugly in a cave or safely high up, and I stuck fluorescent stars on her bedroom ceiling. I slept on a couch in the next room. On our second night in the new apartment, I woke up and heard her crying in bed. I leaped off the couch in the dark, ran a familiar pattern to her bedroom and smashed head first into a wall. I staggered back, then ran into her room, picked her up out of bed and hugged her against my chest, hoping I wasn't bleeding and that she'd never know how it felt to comfort someone while you yourself feel so scared and alone.

Chapter Fifteen:
Universal Studio in Autumn

*T*he piles of leaves alongside the curb are almost as tall as Alex, and as she wades through them, belly-flopping into the largest piles, I follow on the sidewalk. While she dives and laughs, and the last leaves of autumn float down around my head, I suddenly feel dizzy. Last night she wanted to roughhouse with me but I was too tired and finally managed to interest her in a board game. Watching the timer, I realized that for years I've tried to convince myself it's merely an illusion that the sands run faster when they're past the half-way point.

By her own reckoning, she's seven and eleven-quarters years old, and she has begun to ask some hard questions about Harry the Hanukkah Fairy and Santa Claus. The eye doctor, a man not given to metaphysics, says she'll see better with glasses. She is talking less about the wonders of infinity these days and more about plusses and minuses. To make more order in her life, she has posted *Ruls Of My Room* on her door:

no smoking

lisin to wut pepul say

no boys aliud

no kritie [her sensei has told her never to use karate outside of class]

and, at the bottom of the list, Thank You.

After our walk, we go to an ice cream bar, and I watch as she smothers her ice cream under candy sprinkles, chocolate chips, strawberries and hot fudge. The chocolate-vanilla soft serve slowly pirouettes into my own dish like swirls of days and nights, furls of lilies, fingers of dancers touching and drifting apart like smoke. The scent on pillows that lingers after someone has left.

Eventually, if she lives right, she'll be involved in several seductions, in varying roles. Some day she'll no longer unwittingly fall for wine and words, and then hopefully she'll find a new way to let herself enjoy the fall. Being fifty carries its own regrets and pleasures, none of which I can explain to her. I might as well show her a globe and congratulate her for knowing the world. She's been to Universal Studios but hasn't seen the real Universal Studio, which begins with the lazy drift downriver in a snug cradle of bulrushes, until you're eventually delivered into the loving arms of your enemy. If you listen as you float, along the riverbank you can hear whimpers and screams of ecstasy and terror. On the shoreline, the serpent swallows its tail, the phoenix renews itself, and mothers' arms flail below their waists, clutching for their lifelines. Far above, wisps from the whippet fingers of nebulae flick pieces of themselves into the emptiness of space.

At the end, I won't tell her, you leave this world with your own glimmer, swept into the updraft of the universe. You twinkle for an instant, and then you're gone. But not forgotten. Never forgotten. The afterglow stays in someone's eyes. She blinks, and your shadow soaks into her memory.

CHAPTER SIXTEEN:
THE CRASH AT THE ICE SKATING RINK

A year after the divorce was finalized, the joint residential custody in place, and Alex and I had settled in a suburb next to Sandy's, I took her for a beginners' ice skating lesson. I laced up her skates, left her with a group of girls she didn't know who were all waiting for the instructor to call them onto the ice, walked to the other side of the rink, and sat in the bleachers to watch. The instructor skated to the center of the rink and blew his whistle, and as all the girls leaped onto the ice and skated quickly and surely toward him, I saw I'd mistakenly left her with the intermediate class. Helpless, I watched as Alex stepped tentatively onto the ice, fell, and sat on the ice alone, crying. By the time I could reach her, the instructor was comforting her. We brought her over to the beginners' class at the other end of the rink, and I returned to the bleachers.

But the moment I sat back down, it hit me. Blending with Alex, I felt completely helpless and alone in a world in which everyone except me knew everyone else, and everybody knew all the secret rules and how to do everything better than I did. It felt as though all the air had left my body. I knew I was going to cry; I couldn't stop it from coming. I wanted to get to a deserted place, but I literally didn't have the energy to stand. The most I could do was to stop sobbing out loud or shaking, and hope no one noticed me. Sitting in the bleachers, surrounded by strangers, I spent the next hour watching her learn how to skate, enormously grateful for the instructor, who paid her special attention. But as in the Pecos, I'd come to the point where I had nothing left.

I'd had a warning sign a few months earlier but ignored it. At a workshop, a therapist demonstrated how she used movement. She instructed us to just start walking slowly around the room and let our bodies do whatever they wanted. Soon I stopped walking and squatted on my haunches, and suddenly the living room disappeared and I was back in the Pecos. I actually heard the rushing river. As I'd progressively weakened in the Pecos and my feet had blistered, walking had become so painful that I'd begun spending a lot of time in this exact squat.

For several years I had been telling my story about the Pecos as a story of determined survival, laying an inspirational tapestry over the deepest loneliness and helplessness I had ever felt. Alongside my narrative of a trip into the wilderness to the edge of death, where I'd discovered love and the importance of being a father and heroically done what I had to do in order to survive, and then carrying that through the divorce battles and getting Alex settled into her new life, a deeper narrative had been running. I'd screwed up, had made several dumb mistakes that put me into danger. The determined, resourceful me who dug the trench with my hunting knife and buried myself to stay warm enough to survive the night was the same fool who'd gotten into that situation, hadn't brought a good map, had followed an increasingly wild river long after it should have become apparent that I was headed in the wrong direction, didn't follow the first rule of being lost (which I'd known): to stay put and wait for the rescuers. How to explain all that other than by incompetence or maybe some vague death wish?

After I'd returned from the Pecos, my noble narrative held me together: I had survived, and I would survive, to take care of Alex. But at the ice rink, I felt that I'd failed her and had no idea how to find my own way back to anything else that mattered to me. Sitting in the bleachers, watching Alex crying alone on the ice, my narratives flipped. I had no power in the world, nothing to give to my daughter or myself.

I had to find something else with flexible hours so I could take Alex to school, pick her up, take her to friends' houses or be home after school so she could have friends over. But I also needed more money. Throughout my life, whether I'd wanted to ask someone for a favor, or a date, or directions, or where the hardware aisle was in a giant store, I'd struggled to get my courage up. When the rescue team had found me and were rushing through the Pecos river, even as I stood and fell into their arms I felt slightly embarrassed. But desperation can also breed courage, or at least action.

I sat on our bathroom floor so Alex couldn't hear me and phoned Rich Simon at the *Family Therapy Networker*. I'd written an essay a few years ago that the *Networker* published. Now I explained my situation to Rich and said I needed to earn money.

"I really like your writing," he said. "I'll give you an article to write every issue." I had to take a moment to steady my voice.

"Thanks, Rich," I said.

"Welcome to the family," he replied.

For several minutes I remained sitting on the kitchen floor, just taking breaths.

Family Therapy Networker, which changed its name a few years later to *Psychotherapy Networker,* was highly respected in the psychotherapy field. Its 55,000-plus subscribers included psychiatrists, psychologists, social workers, counselors and other mental health professionals. Rich Simon deeply edited every article, and he was as interested in good writing and careful research as in psychotherapy. No writer got away without at least one complete rewrite, usually two, often three. Writers referred to the editing process as getting "simonized," and whenever you emailed a draft and got a call from Rich that began, "Almost there," you knew you were about to get hit with another rewrite.

As an editor, he never let you get away with anything; no careless thinking, toss-off phrase or psychological jargon slipped past him. Occasionally he'd pick out a sentence and ask me what I meant, and I'd have to confess that I didn't really know: I'd been unclear in my own mind and had tried to slip the confusion past myself and Rich and on to the reader. To this day, when my therapy clients describe themselves as co-dependent, depressed, narcissistic or an addict, I tell them I don't know what the word means and have them explain what it means for *them*. Rich was infuriating and kind, accommodating and insistent, and always on target. He kept his promise to me, and in each issue my articles let our readers know about topics ranging from the psychological aftermaths of disasters such as the North Dakota flooding and the Oklahoma City bombing, disgraceful insurance company practices that affected mental health coverage, new research about mental health and treatment, and reasons why diagnostic spikes in conditions like autism, repressed memories, multiple personalities, and childhood bipolar disorder periodically swept across our field.

One day Rich announced that he was going to start a new section of the magazine, "The Clinicians' Digest," a compendium of six or seven articles each issue about the newest trends, research, and controversies affecting psychotherapy and mental health. It was a job that required an understanding of research, something I'd disdained and had steadfastly refused to know anything about. In my MSW program I'd passed Research and Statistics by lying to my professor about being sick for the final and getting hold of the questions before I took the make-up exam. But writing the Digest would finally relieve my anxiety about money, so I took the position and started learning. One good thing about desperation: it can lead to a crash course in learning.

When I began writing "The Clinicians' Digest," I was so intimidated about talking to researchers and major names in psychology—people like psychiatrist Daniel Siegel, international trauma expert Bessel van der Kolk or family therapy pioneer Salvador Minuchin (Minuchin had actually written a classic text book I'd had for one of my graduate classes!)—that despite having a deadline to meet, I would put off making a phone call until the last minute. But as the Digest became more popular and I became more widely known, I got more used to the idea that big people actually wanted to talk to me. Occasionally I addressed controversial topics, and sometimes a respected name in the field would get upset, but my facts were always right. Sometimes *both* sides of an issue would complain to Rich. "If both sides are mad at you, it means you've done your research," Rich told me.

Every year the *Networker* held its Symposium in Washington, DC. One year I was supposed to see Salvador Minuchin at 2 that afternoon, but anti-Iraq War protestors announced a big demonstration in front of the White House. I got up my nerve and told Minuchin about my dilemma.

"You have to go to the demonstration," he told me. "That's more important."

Eventually, people began seeking *me* out, wanting me to write about their work, and as a result two unexpected things happened to my therapy career. I became a better therapist, and as I began to feel more like a therapist and make more contacts in the field, my practice grew. Gradually I came to think of myself as a genuine psychotherapist rather than an iconoclastic outlier.

After I'd been writing "The Digest" for nearly a decade, I started getting waylaid during the Symposiums in the hotel corridors by people who wanted me to write about their work. They were often people more interested in self-promoting than helping the field, so I learned to navigate through the least heavily trafficked corridors in the hotel. I'd still occasionally get snared by someone but by then I was older and used my age to extricate myself. In the incessant hum and buzz of convention noise, with crowds rushing past us while the person went on and on, I'd get a blank look on my face as if my attention had been overwhelmed and wander off. I preferred to think of my technique as selective mutism, not arrogance; I was willing to take the hit for being senile, but not for being rude. I was so pleased with coming up with this technique that I told someone about it.

"You did that to *me,* yesterday," she said. Suddenly I remembered that I had, but I explained —-honestly— that four of us had been talking, and it had been one of the others I'd wanted to get away from.

One year there was a concurrent convention at the hotel, and the news spread that Muhammad Ali was staying there. In an amazing coincidence, on my way to the lobby I got into the elevator on the 10th floor, and the only other person in there was Ali himself, leaning against the back wall. He was already ravaged by Parkinson's, his face heavy and weary. I didn't want to pass up the opportunity to talk to him, but I knew there was nothing I could say that he hadn't heard hundreds of times, and I felt I didn't have the right to burden him with one more dialog of cliché. I nodded when I got in, he gave a weak nod back, and then I turned away from him and faced the elevator door to leave him in peace. But it was *Muhammad Ali*. I kept thinking of *something* meaningful I could say to him, but everything I thought of seemed stale. When we reached the lobby and the elevator doors opened, I glanced back at him and said, "Thanks, Champ." He smiled.

Chapter Seventeen:
The Eternal Flame

When I was diagnosed with prostate cancer, I began wondering whether I'd loved Alex as much as I could have. I've always had this complicated relationship with love and often unrealistic expectations about it. Just like talking about faith, saying the word "love" usually waters it down into banality.

Though I'd like to think that toward the end I salvaged something considerable of my relationship with my father, I never felt that I'd recovered enough of it. When he slipped into his coma with just hours to live, the nurse told me that people in comas can often still hear, and so I whispered something to him. Once Alex asked me what I'd said, but I only weakly paraphrased it; I thought that someday she might find herself beside my deathbed and I wanted her to find her own truth. That would be my final gift to her.

Everyone says "I love you" so much that the phrase is diluted, coated with syrup, and transformed into a Hallmark greeting card; it can get reduced to a tagline we append to our most important relationships. I myself have occasionally said, "I love you" to people in my life just to give reassurance to someone who's asked for it (or to reassure myself) or to bait a hook to snag someone into saying it back. Trying to express love is often like trying to hold smoke.

I almost always say, "I love you," back to Alex when she says it to me, because she's expecting me to say it, and not saying it would give her the idea that I *don't* love her. But it usually feels like I diminish love when I profess it. It's not that I *don't* love her, or that I don't think love's important; I dislike saying I love you because love *is* so important. Love helps us justify our existence. Love is so fundamental that using language to try to describe it diminishes it.

My friend Sharon once told me that she always ended her goodbyes to her son with an, "I love you." Having already lost a son, she said, if either she or her son suddenly died before they saw each other again, she wanted this to be the last words between them. I understand that, but I'm also convinced that saying I love you too often cheapens it. There are plenty of good reasons for saying white lies about other things, but I worry that little white lies about love whittle it away.

Call me an oxymoron, but I'm too much of a romantic to easily say I love you. Some very religious people believe they should never speak the name of God; I believe we should be very careful about naming love aloud. Like God, love's either there or it's not. If it is, you and your loved one know it's there, and verbally acknowledging it too often dilutes it.

So how could I ever locate and describe my love for Alex? Her moods colored mine. I would have risked my life for her and was almost always ready to protect her. (Almost; no one's perfect). I decided on that late afternoon in the Pecos Wilderness to live for her, and when I got my cancer diagnosis, one of my first thoughts was that at least I'd had enough years of raising her to give her a solid head start.

Alex and I touched love together the day I returned from the hospital after my surgery. I'd arranged for her to be well sheltered. My sister had moved into the apartment during my hospital stay, and her godfather Sheldon had flown into town and stayed at a hotel a few blocks away. With everyone at the apartment when I returned, I lay on the couch, nauseous, in pain, hiccupping, a piss-filled catheter bag lying on the floor.

Alex was silent, sullen. That evening as soon as the two adults left her sullenness disappeared, and she made tea for me. I realized that I'd been so worried about making sure she'd been taken care of that I'd sheltered her too much. For some time she'd been trying to act adult, but I'd seen it only as a premature adolescent insistence on being grown up. Now I saw that I should allow her to take care of me and allow myself to be taken care of by her. She brought me tea, and suddenly her eyes teared up. I realized how long it had been since we'd looked into each other's eyes.

"I'm sorry," she whispered, trying to hold her voice steady. At first I thought she meant that she was sorry she was subjecting me to her tears when I was feeling so miserable, but then I realized that her, "I'm sorry" meant a lifetime of other things as well.

"You don't have to apologize for anything," I said. Like her "I'm sorry," my absolution also carried years of meaning. I got myself into an upright position and stretched out my arms and we hugged as well as we could.

So cancer had its upside, another nudge, like my time in the Pecos, to remind me about love. Even though the prognosis was good, death was whispering in my ear to live well, and you can live well by loving. With my cancer, and with her growing up, it was time for me to pay more attention to what was always most important about us, time to do more tending and nurturing to the central flame of our relationship that I'd too seldom noticed dancing in the wind. I vowed to remember that while other people talked and sang and dreamed and wrote about the power and glory of love, I simply needed to remember to stop often and pay attention to what I finally began to trust had always been there.

CHAPTER EIGHTEEN:
BREAKUP AND THE BADLANDS

i

It had been 15 years since the divorce and at the age of 60, I had pretty much accepted that I might never love a woman again, and that seemed okay. I could feel deep communion often enough with Alex, good friends, and therapy clients, and during alone times I meditated, wrote, read, worked out, and played my harmonica in the evenings down by Lake Michigan. Like many single people, I found what I needed, if not often enough to immunize myself from loneliness, at least often enough to feel satisfied with how my life was unfolding. Many times—many times—I would not have traded my single life to gamble finding another lover. Occasionally yearning and aching broke through, but I'd remind myself that this happens even when you're in a relationship. I knew that whether I was single or in a relationship, I'd still find joy, laughter, excitement, and peace and occasional misery

Then, surprisingly—and surprisingly easily—I found someone. The timing was probably no coincidence. Alex was leaving for college, and for the first time in decades I had more time and emotional energy to put into someone else. Maybe, too, with Alex going, I had lost my excuse for playing things safe. It probably helped that my new love lived in New Mexico, half a country away from me; distance can make intimacy safer. For about half a year it was the best love I'd ever had. Years of living and learning about myself and others had finally paid off: I brought into our relationship, and maintained, a more solid sense of myself, of what I wanted, of what I could reasonably expect, and of what I couldn't expect, than I'd ever had before. But eventually, less satisfied with a long distance relationship than I was, she wanted us to continue seeing each other without being exclusive, which felt a little like Blackbeard giving me the freedom to walk wherever I wanted as long as I left the blindfold on, kept my hands tied behind my back, and stepped onto the plank. I knew that I had to end it before things became unpleasant, that it was time to say goodbye while I could still do it without struggling for a different outcome. There was nothing on the horizon but thunderclouds of sorrow and anger.

And so my better way of being in a relationship carried over into our breakup: I walked through the gateway with more gratitude, less anger, and the least self-doubt or blame I'd ever ended a love. We parted on the phone peacefully, mutually acknowledging that we wanted different things from each other than we could give or allow. I knew breaking up would hurt. I expected several weeks of wallowing through the kinds of feelings I'd been avoiding for years, but I figured that at this new stage of my life, with everything I'd learned and with how well we'd ended our time together, I could endure it until the fever broke. After all, severe heartache is mostly an affliction of adolescence.

Two weeks later I suffered the worst emotional crash of my life.

ii

Breaking up and loss happen to all of us, at least a few times in our lives. If you're one of those people who believes that everything happens for a reason—personally, I vacillate between thinking that statement is either sentimental pap or a tautology—I suppose you could say that breakups are a useful way to help acclimate us to mortality. Everything ends. But we individualize the way we grieve, bringing our personal themes into play and hiring our own discordant band to accompany us on the death march. The blueprints of our plans and dreams change from building something new to shoring up the sinking foundation of the house we no longer want to live in. We miss our lovers terribly, want them to miss us, want their lives to remain frozen at the moment of breakup, want them back under satisfying terms or want them to suffer, want to rewrite the final moments and conversations and write future dialogs of revenge or of reconciliation. We sift through the ashes for clues, irrationally hoping we'll find something that will help us reconcile, provide justification or meaning for what happened, or give us more wisdom and immunity for the next relationship.

A few nights after we broke up, I rode the el back home from my office, heading into an unusually colorful sunset for Chicago. The thought struck me that in rural New Mexico I saw such sunsets almost daily, flaming and panoramic, dwarfing everything built by humans. Depression slammed into me hard. Battening down the hatches in advance of the storm I felt coming,

I deleted Google Earth from my computer so I wouldn't look at her house.

I decided that I needed to go for the ultimate cure: I would have to wait a few months until I regained some footing, and then I would go on my first hitchhiking trip in almost 30 years. I emailed a producer at our local NPR station. She liked my work, and in the last year I'd recorded a few essays for her, for free, so I felt I could ask one small favor. "I'm going on a hitchhiking trip in August," I wrote, "and I think there will be some great pieces to come out of it. But I've never recorded anything outside of your studio, and I'd like to get some technical info from you." Then I poured a stiff shot of Jack Daniels, forced myself to sip it slowly and went to bed with the television on, choosing mediocre company over myself. When the storm's bad enough, you go for any escape. In younger breakup days, I'd occasionally slept with women I didn't especially want to be with.

The producer emailed me that she'd look at my essays when I got back but she wouldn't promise me anything, and she couldn't loan me any equipment. The elevator cables suddenly snapped. Furious, I started to email back that I hadn't asked for any equipment, only advice about recording, and she'd never see any essays from me again. At the last second I remembered the rule about waiting a few hours before sending off an angry email.

That night, I lay in bed trying to fall asleep and slipped into a fugue-like state in which I clearly saw me lying in my bathtub and cutting my wrists. I watched myself calmly, with only a faint alarm sounding, like when you hear your neighbor's alarm clock muffled by the walls. It was as if the vision was issuing from a cave inside me that I hadn't known about. Although I knew I'd never do it, the clarity of the vision scared me.

I wondered why this particular breakup had hit so much harder than others. Maybe the better the relationship, the worse the breakup. Losing my first love in 15 years had surely intensified the loss. Maybe I had that nagging late middle age illusion that time was running out and that I might have no more chances to get love right. Maybe the depression and anxiety was an old unpaid debt coming due: when I'd gone through the divorce with Sandy, I'd had other concerns to occupy me: desperate strategizing and legal battles, setting up a new home for Alex, and then protecting and raising her. Now, with nothing to distract me, I felt like a man who'd escaped from prison, breathed freedom, and suddenly found himself thrown into solitary confinement for trying to escape. But while all those explanations helped explain the suicidal fugue, I knew they didn't quite get at it.

My anger at the NPR producer gave me the key; I'd learned from therapy that when I have such a volatile reaction, some historical nerve has been laid bare. By all rights, my mother , who had batted only about .175 when it came to letting me know she loved me, shouldn't have even been in the major leagues. So I'd learned early to be ashamed to want or ask for love and to blame myself when I didn't get it. Now when my ex-lover told me she couldn't give me the love I'd asked for, a toxic sluice of old shame rushed in: I was to blame for having expected something more.

And something else too: the day before my suicidal fugue, an old memory from a fishing trip with my father had suddenly flared. I was about seven years old. A school of small fish had found our spot, and we'd spent a considerable amount of time carefully removing the hooks from their mouths or gills and setting them back into the water. But one small fish completely swallowed the hook. I kept trying gently to remove it, until finally the fish started thrashing. Finally there was nothing to do but yank the hook hard. The fish gasped in my hand, its guts coming up through its throat.

The breakup had hooked me in my guts. Now every time I enjoyed something I'd imagine she was beside me sharing it, or I'd plan to tell her all about it. A movie I'd chosen as pure escapism took place in, of all places, New Mexico. You could make a case for my having unconsciously chosen that movie—maybe I'd read in some review that it had been filmed there—but in the two next days, twice I overheard people talking about moving to New Mexico. Then someone mentioned his dog and, conversing on depressed automatic pilot, not really caring about him or his damn dog, I asked what breed it was. It was the same breed as her dog, an Australian shepherd—a breed I'd never heard of before we'd dated.

iii

The hard truth about healing, physically or psychically, is that it always happens more slowly and unevenly than we'd like. The old notion of needing to go through the five stages of grief has been replaced; the current paradigm in grief work is that instead of thinking about how to eventually leave your grief behind, you learn to walk with it. When I finally began to feel a little better and thought that I could endure some time alone, I decided to drive 14 hours to the Badlands. I know a place there so still and silent that you literally can't hear a sound—no wind or breeze, no crickets, no solitary bird call—one of the few completely silent places left on our planet.

Sometime during the long drive to the Badlands, I began missing her terribly. I kept imagining her sitting in the car with me, kept wanting to talk to her, and I fought the impulse across Wisconsin and Minnesota. Finally, in those rolling treeless hills of South Dakota, I realized that I *needed* her to be there, and that I would be okay if she was, so I invited her to ride along in the car. For the first time since our breakup, I allowed myself to see her clearly—her eyes, her smile. Just as I'd literally talked with myself alongside the riverbank in the Pecos, I allowed her voice inside my head. I nodded hi, smiled back at her, and telepathically told her she was welcome to stay and visit. We had a good time talking, noting the scenery, watching for speed traps, reminiscing. A few times she suddenly said something mean, and I retaliated with those kinds of insults that only people who have been intimate with each other can come up with. Then I realized that the hurtful things she said were coming from me—after all, I was writing our conversation. In a convoluted self-protective way, I'd made her say those things because I was enjoying our time together in the car so much that I needed to save me from getting hurt again.

"It's amazing, the things we do to protect ourselves," I said, and we both laughed.

The first time I'd driven across South Dakota I hadn't even spotted the Badlands, though they're just about 10 miles south of the Interstate. They don't loom dramatically on the horizon. Created by erosion, they're mainly below it, like a trap door into the earth's unconscious. Most people who go to the Badlands drive along its scenic roads and get out of their cars only to stand at designated overlooks, or walk on the few short looped trails. But when you wander off the trails, you can leave the world and disappear inside the silence and phantasmagorical landscapes.

So I parked my car, left a trail, and wandered deeper into the Badlands. Eventually I found the right place where I could sit out of the hot sun: the base of a butte sloped to form a backrest at a perfect angle and was sheltered from any occasional breeze so that the only sound I could hear was my breathing. I occasionally felt my blood pulsing through my ears. I meditated, dozed, sat, stretched, wrote, read *The Odyssey*, lay prone. I watched the distant buttes and studied nearby weeds. Once, disappointed, I thought I heard a distant semitruck and then thought no, it must be an airplane and then saw it was just a fly buzzing past my ears. As the sun drifted lower, I decided to bring some heat into my life and found a new spot where the sun warmed my shoulders and arms. Eventually the sun dropped behind the hills and sunset colors spread wide across the sky, the same colors that Homer called dawn's fingertips of rose.

I put on my sweatshirt, watched the swirling sky colors and how they played on the rocks and hillsides. When the first stars appeared. I stretched out on my back and stared up into the deepening night sky until it became sequined with stars. Eventually it occurred to me that I hadn't once invited her to sit with me. I breathed deeply and thought: I'm free.

CHAPTER NINETEEN:
THE RETURN OF THE EXERCISE

It took several years before I fell in love again. I wrote, I built up my therapy practice, and I found my way back to genuinely enjoying doing things by myself without feeling like I was merely making the best of a temporary situation. I swam in calmer waters. Eventually I decided to start dating again, more out of want than need, and Lynn and I found each other.

We went together almost ten years, and it reconfigured my life as much as my marriage to Sandy had. I still lived in the same apartment in Oak Park where Alex and I had spent our lives since the divorce almost twenty years ago, and Lynn had a condo in Chicago. Since Alex had left for college, my apartment had served more as an office and a place to eat and sleep than a home, and that was sufficient. But with Lynn, the center of my life shifted. I stayed in her condo Fridays through Tuesday mornings until we finally broke up. Getting wiser about yourself and relationships doesn't make breaking up any easier.

It's the evening after we've broken up. Uncertain whether I'd finally quit or been fired, and having gotten through the next day and into twilight better than expected, I've decided to test myself to see whether I can go beyond not-shattered into actually enjoying myself. So I'm sitting on a bench in a fairly secluded place in the park, intending to leisurely spend the evening people watching and to run that exercise which I'd discovered over four decades ago when I was about 25.

Throughout the years I'd run lighter versions of it, occasionally sitting outside coffee shops and trying to meet people's eyes. But when cell phones took over our culture I had fewer opportunities to try it; strangers, and I, now had a handy excuse to avoid connecting. When you're more insulated, you face fewer tests, a mixed blessing.

In the park tonight instead of cell phones, dogs on leashes provide cover. For all of us, paying attention to the dogs feels safer than making eye contact. That's fine, I remind myself. This evening is for relaxation and fun, not for testing myself. My people watching's a game in which there's no scoring, no winners or losers. Something to play just for the hell of it. I'm here tonight to feel better than I felt earlier today, glad to know our relationship's tipping point is no longer ahead of me but in the rear view mirror. I'll take *fait accompli* over anxiety any day. Whether you're safely back inside your hotel room or flooded with adrenaline as you plummet, it's better to get off the edge of the ledge.

Here in the park the cicadas have just emerged, thousands of them chirping away, looking for, well, not quite love but a related intoxication. After lying underground for 13 years they've dug themselves out and are calling to each other to get it on, rubbing their legs together and wriggling their butts and wings. In just a few weeks, at the end of their lovefest they'll all die. Some will die even before they're completely sated: during the days of orgy, even the gentle robins turn into hawks and buzzards and feast on them. Another 17 years from now the orphans of the love-in will emerge for *their* mortality ball.

I'm not sure the cicadas have the best approach to love. I've spent many of my years searching for something more complex. But tonight I know what I want: simplicity. Sitting on the bench thinking about nothing in particular, not so much to avoid thinking about her but instead going for the Zen of calm curiosity and emptiness. Lost in thought, I barely notice this couple walk past me with their dog, a big one who brushes against me.

"Sorry," she says.

I think, "Actually I was only disturbed by your apologizing for something you didn't need to apologize for." But on a night like this—perfect temperature, a crescent moon slicing through clouds like a scythe— why get upset by something so minor? I just smile and wave my hand in an it's OK gesture, but they've already passed me and are too much into each other to notice. Then the guy calls back to me: "Nice evening, isn't it?" The only reason he felt he had to say anything at all was because he either wanted to announce his turf or to support her as she apologized. Sir Galahad as the village idiot. It didn't have anything to do with concern for *me*.

I wait for the next passerby, slip back into enjoying the evening. The cicadas aren't the only ones to have come out of hiding. Recently having emerged from the pandemic miasma, people are strolling around still getting used to being back among others. We're remembering that we no longer have to automatically head to the other edge of the sidewalk to keep social distance. We've tentatively gotten used to no longer thinking each person who comes near us is a potential infector. Masks have gradually dropped away.

If there is ever a propitious time to break up, which of course there isn't, this is it. I realize that for the first time this summer I'm allowing myself to notice the fireflies. Gentle beacons, slow amorous blimps, fuzzy mating semaphores. A mosquito bites my arm. It would be just my luck if, having avoided Covid, this mosquito's given me West Nile virus. It's good to know that my humor's still deflecting the blinding light of self-interrogation that a breakup can pin you under: the odds that any mosquito cruising around biting people is carrying West Nile virus are so small that my thought really was 90% humor and only 10% morose anxiety, a good indication of how well I'm doing. But as long as the mosquito has momentarily disrupted my mood, if I take just a moment to reassure myself that there are no ticks on the bench possibly carrying Lyme disease I'll be able to get back more quickly into contemplative relaxation.

Tick check done, I drift back into the zone. I breathe slowly and deeply in, breathe slowly and completely out, which I can do now that there's not swarms of Covid virus floating around. In one of the troughs between the waves of cicada singing, I hear two birds twitter, hidden in different spots in a tree. Are they just glad to be there, singing to themselves? Is one singing to the other? Here comes a solo woman walking a medium size dog, both of them clearly enjoying their walk. They're in synch. She's letting it sniff around and go off the path into the weeds, snuffling and occasionally lifting his leg. A good life, spending your time prospecting and always finding some pheromones interesting enough to add in your own scent, untroubled either by thoughts of rejection or of hopes that another dog will pick up on your scent and come looking for you. You do what you do just because you do it. As an extra bonus, there's someone behind you cleaning up your mess.

"I love how you're letting your dog explore," I say to her. She smiles. It lights me up so much I quickly look away, and they pass on.

In their wake the cicadas crescendo again. Through the cicadas' noise, I hear the birds in the tree still singing. Romance is wonderful because it happens so rarely. A serenader and a lover smoldering in the night. With crows in heat, the same intent but different music. She may already be on the hunt while I'm sitting in the park just trying to make fleeting eye contact with strangers. If Lynn were watching me right now, it would be nice if she were hoping I'd meet someone tonight: I'd rather be bathed in her benevolence or watered by her sorrow than targeted by her malevolence. Even better, I'd rather not be thinking about her at all. But when someone gets a limb lopped off, for some time afterward the brain still feels the phantom limb hanging around.

I'm doing it again. Instead of cultivating calm here in the park, I'm manufacturing thoughts that turn into parasites that chew on my liver. I'm forgetting that I'm here tonight to just play a game. Morose and angry thoughts don't get you anywhere, not tonight, not ever. Telling other people and even yourself why a relationship ended is a useless exercise. Each person has their own story. Breakup narratives lack balance, mutual accountability. Let her have her story; I'm too magnanimous to want her to leave our relationship empty-handed. By walking away from fights, I'd shown restraint, quiet strength. Only people who need to pick fights label pacifism as weakness or passive aggressiveness. But her explanation about our breakup may not put me in such a good light, and it will shape my image in others' eyes. It's a little like knowing a madman's finger is on the nuclear button.

"You're always looking for what might go wrong," she said, missing the fact that my proactiveness was a counterweight to her optimistic obliviousness. "You don't stand up for yourself," she said, not appreciating that my retreats often saved us from raging at each other. Chief Joseph of the Nez Perce spoke the most graceful surrender line in history: "I will fight no more forever." He lived a long life. Muhammad Ali used rope-a-dope to beat George Foreman: he kept backing up against the ropes and covering up until Foreman exhausted himself beating against Ali's defenses.

But tonight's not about winning or losing. It's about healing. I've chosen a perfect spot, on the only semi-secluded path in the park. An automatic sorting: people on the main path are heading somewhere, but the ones walking past me on this quiet path walk more slowly, are more focused on each moment. Another couple with their dog approaches. I smile, though now it's almost too dark for them to see it, and say, "Great dog walk, isn't it?" They walk past me and then pause a few yards away, knowing they should respond. "So many of these fireflies," she says. "It's beautiful," and they keep walking. She has an accent I can't place.

They're far enough away so we're at a safe distance from getting entrapped in conversation, so I call out, "Where you from?"

"Australia," she answers, and they continue walking but, probably aware that a one word answer feels a bit rude, she pauses while her dog sniffs at something. "We don't have fireflies in Australia," she calls back.

I reply, "But you have some of the deadliest snakes and spiders in the world."

"Yeah, it's true," she laughs and they keep walking. He never says a word.

It just may turn out tonight that this mellow I'm trying to stoke up is closer to a sociopath's reassuring smile than to a genuine benevolence. More West Nile humor of mine. I'm certainly not interested in destroying anything, except maybe any burgeoning relationship of hers that starts up between now and a few weeks after I've made a better start to get beyond feeling crappy, which I thought was already beginning to happen, but apparently not. Had she already started looking for someone better, or was she just focused on wiping the dogshit of our years off her shoe? Or is she grieving?

Like most people, too often we both avoided dealing with things that troubled us about the other, about our relationship. Evasiveness has so many different flavors. There's fearful evasiveness, strategic evasiveness, and unconscious evasiveness. We'd spent months cultivating our private wild gardens. At some point there's not much you can do about that except try to let it go, which is its own kind of evasiveness. Dig a deep enough pit and eventually you can't escape. I look down the darkening path to see whether anyone else is headed toward me.

PART FOUR:
GRIEF, MEMORIES, NOSTALGIA

The Chest of Memories

We all have our memories. Sometimes we lock them away, even from ourselves. Sometimes we haul them out for ourselves or for others. Over the years, we occasionally—deliberately or half-consciously—remember our treasure chest and rummage through it. Along with the jewels, there are spiders and an occasional dusty mouse turd. Be glad you still have the treasure chest and it's not just a sterile display case.

Chapter Twenty:
Blue New Orleans

By the time hurricane Katrina had devastated New Orleans, I hadn't been back for a long time, the longest Chicago-New Orleans gap since my first visit there almost thirty years ago. Almost all my friends, including Gordon, had gradually moved away, and Mardi Gras had begun to seem like a party for younger people and a dispiriting attempt for older people to try to prove or resurrect something. After Katrina, there seemed even less reason to return. Fourteen months after Katrina flooded 80 percent of the city, the population of New Orleans had sunk to about 190,000—down from 450,000.

Siren calls may fade, but they seldom disappear. After Katrina I began thinking more often about the first time I'd gone there when I was 23, had no money, responsibilities or plan and had imagined New Orleans suffused with a soft blue light, a dream place of undefined possibilities and open chances. So almost a year and a half after Katrina, having recovered from cancer and with Alex in the home stretch of high school, I finally decided to fly down for a visit, thinking it was time to take stock of New Orleans and of myself. When the plane began its descent I surprised myself: my eyes began to tear.

I left my suitcase at the hotel, this time a decent place instead of a skid row flophouse, headed immediately for Jackson Square and sat on a bench where over the years I'd spent hours watching, talking, and melding into a different life. At a certain age, memories begin to feel like faded daguerreotypes, fossilized anecdotes. We know this in our dreams but forget it in our waking hours: our lifetime on Earth isn't just an accretion of moments and years, but a membrane. Sitting in Jackson Square all those years later, frozen memories thawed, began to smoke, glow. I thought about that girl who got on the train in Jackson, Mississippi, sat next to me and introduced me, when I was so anxious and naïve, to the kinds of possibilities that New Orleans can offer if you just put yourself out there to receive them. In the carelessness of youth, I never took her number, never asked her last name, and I never saw her again. Now sitting on the bench in Jackson Square thirty-seven years later, I wondered whether she'd stayed in

New Orleans, survived Katrina or something else, and I stepped through time and thanked her for something I couldn't have known then, that with the start she gave me, New Orleans had seeped permanently into my life.

New Orleans, the domain of the jazz funeral and a city resonant with hundreds of years of sorrow and joy, had always been able to party and laugh in the face of adversity, but now the frivolity and gaiety were missing. The city was weary, still shocked; there was no lilt in it. A veteran dentist told me that since Katrina he'd made more jaw protectors for people who were grinding their teeth than he'd made in his entire career. There were fewer artists around Jackson Square and more fortune tellers. You didn't have to wait in line for coffee and beignets at Café du Monde. On Royal Street, the owner of Alpine stood outside, asking the few people who strolled past whether they'd like to look at his menu. Bourbon Street was just a hollow echo of itself, a street of ghosts; you could walk from one end to the other without once maneuvering around anyone. The mule-drawn carriages on Decatur Street alongside Jackson Square used to take up the entire block; now there were only two of them. In the devastated lower Ninth

Ward, where even street signs had been washed away, people had tacked up pieces of wood or cardboard with the street names scrawled on them. In a disaster of a lesser magnitude, they'd have decorated the signs with Mardi Gras beads or made up their own street names. Instead, on one sagging wooden house, someone had spray painted in black, "Please send donations to help me rebuild," and there was a phone number with a Houston area code.

We too easily evoke the theme of resilience in the wake of disaster. Sometimes people survive simply because they don't know what else to do. Now feeling old at 60, sitting in Jackson Square, I was no longer sure what resilience meant to me, of what proportions of denial and acceptance, of action, resignation and rumination comprised it. In my youth, resilience had boiled down to this: I could continue something or quit, and no matter which I chose, I knew that I could probably call on it at any time. Like oil, the reserves seemed unlimited.

Returning to New Orleans in the wake of Katrina, feeling old, worn down, I feared that the New Orleans I knew would never return. I tried to reassure myself by thinking that holding on to anything too tightly squeezes the life out of it. Ever since they'd removed my cancerous prostate, I knew how the Indians felt when the first white men showed up in their hills: they chased the intruders out, but they never again felt the same when they looked at the horizon. Sitting on the bench, I remembered my 20's and 30's in New Orleans and Chicago when every orgasm felt like I could go as high as I wanted, multiple times. When aches and pains reminded me in a good way that I was alive—signs of repair going on, not the harbingers of worse things to come. I remembered when optimism was a gateway to the future, not a survival strategy for getting through the present.

I thought how at various points in our lives our memories, experiences, plans and hopes carry a different value and a different tariff. As we age, we sometimes try to romanticize our past or narrow our future, become our own hagiographer, start thinking about our eulogy. Meanwhile the road still unfolds, even while the imperatives to stay closer to home, press flowers into our scrapbook and hoard nuts for the winter grow stronger. Recently I'd bought long-term health care insurance.

Sitting in Jackson Square, I tried to sell myself on the idea that before I ended up in a nursing home, I'd put on a backpack one last time, walk to a highway, stick out my thumb and start a farewell tour around the country, revisiting one last time places and old acquaintances who had drifted away, stopping in other cities to visit long-time friends, and that I'd finish my travels in New Orleans, where my adult adventures began. Once in my hitchhiking days, I saw an old man with a scraggly white beard and a small, beat-up suitcase standing on the side of the road, thumb out. I felt sorry for him even while I admired his freedom but, too full of my own youth, I passed the opportunity to walk up to him and talk; I was in too much of a hurry to get to where I was going. Now I'd almost arrived.

Tuning into my own particular song of resilience, I tried to remember, to hope, that for New Orleans and for me, our greatest vulnerabilities fuel both our denial and our hope. Below sea level, with the Louisiana bayous that protect New Orleans from Gulf hurricanes eroding each year, New Orleans exists in a swamp where everything grows, and I hoped that in some unpredictable way the city would grow again.

Finally I got up from my Jackson Square bench and walked down to Maspero's. A waitress in her early 20's, blue ribbons in her hair and a blue tattoo between her shoulder blades, told me that she'd arrived almost a year ago to help in the relief effort. She'd fallen in love with the city and decided to stay—it's that easy when you're young—and for a moment I felt in love again too, with the city, with her, and with myself, here, in this way, on this soft evening, because of who I was, because of decisions I'd made and adventures I'd chosen. And then I felt it again, a flicker of the old New Orleans magic. I didn't need to follow the tyranny of clocks and calendars; I could still choose my own measurements for how much time I'd lived and how much remained. Sitting by Jackson Square, or wandering to the levee and watching the Mississippi River flow, or walking in and out of the shadows of the French Quarter, I could still stand outside of time, still feel memory's sparks.

Chapter Twenty-one:
Slipping Past New Year's Eve

I used to measure a successful New Year's Eve by how well I avoided midnight. After a lot of rough ones in my teens and twenties, eventually I learned how to slip past the sleeping dragon. So on one New Year's Eve without a girlfriend and still shaking off my divorce, I stuck with my usual safe regimen. First, I planned to catch a 4:45 movie downtown, ahead of the flood of New Year's Eve couples. All these couples in love change the feeling inside the theater and affect the viewing of the movie, so I planned to get in and get out before they arrived. A few New Year's Eves before I'd married, I'd chosen an Australian supernatural slasher movie, the 11 PM showing. I figured that because no one wanted to be inside the theatre at midnight, the 11 PM start time would fumigate the place of lovers. And in fact, the only other person in the theater sat a few rows behind me and off to the left, wearing a dark trench coat. I usually exit theaters through the exit doors up in front, on the side of the screen. It gives me an illicit thrill. But I decided to walk out the normal way this time. What if

I took the deserted back exit and this guy followed me and was either naked under his trench coat or concealing a machete?

This particular year, because I was finally earning decent money, I planned to cap off the early movie by returning home and opening the most expensive bottle of wine I'd ever bought and savoring it. After a rigorous and intriguing test—would the really expensive wine actually taste better than my usual $7.99 bottles?—I'd be in bed long before midnight, wearing earplugs.

Things began perfectly. It was a freezing late afternoon, but I caught the el quickly. I like to get stoned right before the movie starts, so at 4:55 (I wanted to eliminate the trailers), I entered the multiplex pleasantly stoned and rode the long slow escalator up toward the box office, feeling like Louis XIV on *le grande promenade*. Then—because everything at the multiplex is overdone—I zigzagged through the labyrinthine ropes they'd set up to the box office for the crowds who hadn't shown up yet, feeling as foolish as a rat in a maze. Finally, I strolled up to the bored teenager behind the window, who'd been watching me navigate for what seemed like several minutes. "One for *Wrestler*," I said

"You want the 7:45?" he asked.

Why would I want the 7:45? I thought. Had they actually trained him to hustle the more expensive showing?

"No, the one that's just starting."

"There isn't one just starting," he said. I looked at the electronic show times, and sure enough no 4:45 showing was posted for *Wrestler*. The newspaper had been wrong. I thought for the first time that maybe the death of newspapers wasn't such a bad thing. A safe New Year's Eve was suddenly *not* working out. I had ridden the el downtown and now had to walk back to it and go home movieless and figure out some way to kill several hours before it was late enough to have my glass of wine and go to bed. As I exited the multiplex right into the teeth of a nasty wind, I vowed to walk slowly, trying to distract myself from the freezing weather by observing everything. I told myself that if Tibetan monks can sit outside in thin robes and meditate while the winds howl down from Everest, I could take a slow stoned walk through downtown Chicago. But even if I walked slowly to the el, I'd be home by 6:00, too soon to uncork the wine.

I tried my time-honored antidote against a New Year's Eve depression spiral by reminding myself that New Year's Eve is a meaningless date; calendars are artificial contrivances, and every physicist and Buddhist knows that time isn't linear or segmented. I remembered much worse New Year's Eves. Tonight's was just a light head cold. One evening I'd waited in a snowstorm on a street corner for semi-friends to show up, sitting on a fire hydrant, and by the time I realized they'd changed their plans, I was covered with snow, my elbows on my knees, chin in hands, looking like a frosted version of Rodin's Thinker. Finally, I'd trudged four miles through calf-deep snow to a club where an ex-lover barmaid friend was working, making it there, frozen, my feet soaked, at 11:30. Unable to endure hanging out inside the place, especially at midnight—it was called Xanadu, in case you like irony—I got her car keys and sat in her car. Finally at 1:15 AM she showed up, we drove to her apartment and had joyless sex, and after a few hours' sleep I snuck out of her bed and outside into a subzero New Year's morning thinking with morose gratefulness that I had one entire year before the next New Year's Eve.

Then in this late afternoon review of New Year's Eves, I suddenly remembered one nearly 40 years ago with my oldest friend, Mary, my former undergrad professor of English Lit. In those days I hadn't yet learned that I could relate to professors as human beings, but twice after I graduated, when I was in the backwash of crises and broke, Mary let me live in her big suburban house. She always assumed I could be a writer, even when I doubted it myself. We made no demands on each other, and we lived together so easily that even our silences felt comfortable. My only obligation was to accompany her on Sundays when she took her senescent mother to lunch. Indian Trails restaurant catered to a genteel lunchtime geriatric clientele, so I had to wear a tie and sport coat. Although I managed to scrounge up a tie, I used a paper clip for a tie clip. One day, after I had been living with Mary for nearly a year, we ran into some people I knew and I introduced Mary as my former English professor. That evening she told me, "I'm not your English professor. I'm your friend."

We both dreaded December 31, so we spontaneously decided to have an un-New Year's Eve by going to a 4 PM matinee, eating dinner at a neighborhood Chinese restaurant with placemats keyed to a different yearly cycle, and making sure we were home and in our bedrooms by 10 PM. The movie was a perfect choice. The theater, in its last days, had a leaking ceiling with a water spot than ran down the screen, and the ambience and the Jackie Chan movie were so awful that we laughed about sitting there on New Year's Eve. It stopped New Year's Eve cold, like a backfire stops a forest fire. The evening worked so well that we did it the next year too, though we couldn't find a movie quite as bad.

Mary had earned her aversion to New Year's Eves. Several decades before I met her, when she was somewhere in her 20's and deeply in love, she'd miscarried a short time before her due date, her first child, and a week later her husband suddenly shocked her by walking out of her life. She mentioned this incident to me once, only once, and although she never said this, I understood by piecing together other things she told me over the years that she never again fell into that kind of passionate love. If you feel you have to, you can lock up a chamber of your heart and still live well.

In today's freezing late afternoon, it surprised me to remember that I'd gotten this idea about navigating New Year's Eves with Mary. Before her death seven years ago, she'd been steadily deteriorating in both body and mind, and for the last six months of her life I'd briefly talked with her only once or twice on the phone. I'd been aware of feeling a considerable amount of guilt for staying away; this evening, finally, I understood she'd been so important to me that seeing her decline had been more than I could bear.

We talk about warm memories as though they're a synesthetic trope, but I realized I'd been walking slowly for several blocks and no longer felt cold. I passed several downtown beautiful people bars with big windows that let passers-by see what a great time everyone inside was having, and I knew that I was on the better side of the windows. The energy at parties always seems so out of kilter with what works for me, the difference between sipping a warm midnight cognac while a Haydn quartet's on the stereo, or puking up a dozen cans of Miller in the midst of a disco hurricane. I found an out of the way bar outside of downtown Chicago that was practically empty—give me a red neon Budweiser clock instead of a glittering disco ball—and I sat there nursing a beer and thinking about more times with Mary until the local New Year's Evers started to filter in, and then I left.

Later, on my walk home from the el station, I did what had recently become a habit. I cut diagonally through a small churchyard, and I realized that almost every time I did it, I wondered whether, because the path curves first one direction then the other, I actually saved any steps. This evening I laughed about doing the kind of calculations that crab my soul and then I noticed how the soft courtyard lighting created my shadow on the building's wall, how it grew and shrank as I walked, like a companion, a shade. Like my own flickering capacity for intimacy which made me miss my good friend only years after she had died.

When I got home, I poured the wine, let it breathe, took off my shoes, put on some Schumann lieder, and tasted the wine. Schumann knew the music of sorrow and love. I thought about how we can spend so much of our lives constructing a cage around our hearts and then, if we live right, in our later years the heat of our heart slowly melts the bars until one day they become the throbbing veins on its surface. This New Year's Eve wine, I noticed, was meant for leisurely sipping, careful tasting, had body and flavor, a swirl of sweet and bitter, much fuller than my usual cheap stuff.

CHAPTER TWENTY-TWO:
GIVING UP THE REINS

When I was working on an article for *The Net-worker* about equine-assisted psychotherapy, I called up a therapist who used horses as co-therapists in his work with troubled adolescents and their families. While we were talking, I mentioned that my eight-year old daughter loved horses, but that we lived in a Chicago suburb. Doug invited Alex and me to his home in rural Colorado. I wouldn't have accepted the invitation except for Alex: the divorce was still fresh, and to consolidate the custody arrangement I wanted to give her the kinds of adventures she'd never get with her mother. Neither Sandy nor I were feeling secure enough yet about how our futures with our daughter would work out.

Because we'd never find his house, nestled in the foothills of the Sangre de Cristo Mountains, we planned to meet him in a weedy parking lot beside an abandoned gas station/cafe and follow him along miles of labyrinthine gravel and dirt roads. He drove up in a battered pickup truck with a cracked windshield, a huge mastiff sitting alongside him, its drool wetting down the stuffing that seeped through the cracks in the truck's upholstery. Alex, growing up in a comfortably liberal suburb in the Midwest flatlands, had never seen anything like this.

"You wanna ride with me or your dad?" Doug asked.

I was surprised but pleased when she ran over and climbed into his truck. I'd often considered many of her friends' parents over-protective and had been proud about letting her take more chances. Any anxiety this had caused me had seemed a reasonable price to pay for helping her develop the confidence to step out into the world and explore. It built trust between us. If you keep too tight a rein on your kid, when the inevitable day comes for her to step out on her own—a day that, despite every parent's fantasy, never comes when you choose it—she'll be less prepared.

That afternoon, Doug took Alex to a small round pen to get acquainted with Buddy, a big, high-strung, unpredictable horse, whom he described as a "perpetual adolescent." Alex had previously known only amusement park horses that walked around dirt packed circles while thinking about feedbags. Standing next to Buddy was the difference between watching a tiger caged in a zoo and smelling its breath in the jungle.

Doug taught Alex how to "join" with Buddy. She walked him in circles with a short rope. He told her that whenever Buddy tested her by stopping, she should give a gentle tug, and if that didn't work, she should tug more firmly. Soon, she found the zone in which both she and Buddy felt reassured and knew who was in charge.

With the proper relationship established, Alex dropped the rope and used just hand signals to get Buddy walking, cantering, and reversing directions. Then she rode him bareback around the pen, with her arms stretched out to her sides and her eyes closed, feeling his rippling muscles with her thighs and communicating to him with gentle leg pressure. She was getting in touch with the power and sensitivity of horses, and her own as well.

Then Doug invited me into the pen to take hold of the rope and walk Buddy around with Alex on his back. I was worried. What if Buddy sensed my nervousness, got skittish, bolted, and bucked Alex off? Horses, being prey animals, are highly sensitive to people around them, and sure enough Buddy started to nicker and balk. "Don't be scared," I said to Alex, recognizing that the anxiety in my voice completely belied my words.

"I'm *not* scared," she said, clearly annoyed at me.

Feeling rebuked and humiliated, the least comfortable person in the corral, I saw that in dealing with my nervousness by trying to reassure *her*, I was making things worse for both of us. I looked helplessly at Doug, who laughed. In that moment I understood the power of equine-assisted family therapy.

In the coming months, as the lesson resonated, I understood that I'd long been giving Alex mixed signals by combining messages of freedom with expressions of fear. "You can step out into the world," I'd been telling her, thinking I'd been exuding and imparting calm confidence, but my tone and attitude had actually conveyed, "Be afraid." This double message didn't fit my image of my parenting style at all, and I didn't like it.

We visited Doug every summer for the next ten years. He and his wife Dawn became Alex's aunt and uncle. Alex and Doug went on daylong rides across prairies, through arroyos, and over mountains. Once while they sat on their horses calmly admiring a view, Buddy suddenly saw a rattlesnake and started, throwing Alex. She hit the ground so hard she lost her breath, and it took a few seconds before she could recover. Doug watched to see what she'd do. When she walked over to Buddy and remounted, she noticed with surprise that his eyes had teared up.

Doug had once been a high-priced, fast-living therapist in Miami Beach. He had a black belt in karate, and was a horseman, a cowboy, an expert marksman, and a certified snowboarding instructor. Long before that, he'd been a short, skinny, vulnerable, angry, and terrified child, beaten by his bipolar father and bullied by the kids in his school. Doug was bipolar too—and when Alex was 16, his mania took over.

A few months after we last saw him in the summer of 2007, he quit his therapy practice and joined a private security force in Qatar. His marriage in irreparable tatters, he returned with fierce tattoos, cracked ribs, and a bruised spleen, telling contradictory stories about what had happened. He began a mad odyssey to Louisiana and Florida, sending out bizarre text messages and e-mails. Deeply depressed and flat broke, he returned to Colorado and got a job at the local prison, but he didn't show up for work the first day—and then he disappeared. I tried to prepare Alex for what I believed was coming.

A few days later, the sheriff's department found Doug's body in the snow on the mountainside of a closed down ski resort. I struggled to figure out how to tell Alex, but couldn't think of any good way. I finally just said, "They found Doug's body." She turned and ran into her room, slamming the door, and I stood in the living room listening to her cry, trying to figure out what to do. I felt as helpless as I had that afternoon when she'd first mounted Buddy. I'd always considered myself an excellent therapist and father, but now I was just an impotent fraud who'd clumsily blurted out that one of the most important males in her life was dead.

Eventually, I remembered what Doug and Buddy had taught me: I needed to trust Alex to deal with things. I'd wanted to overprotect her; to break the news in a way that she wouldn't cry, wouldn't feel the loss too much. It was time to remember that Alex could take care of herself.

While she cried in her room, she wrote Doug a long

e-mail, telling him everything he'd meant to her. She called friends. During the next days and months, she digested the news in the way of mourners since human time began: unevenly, unsurely, reluctantly, slowly.

When we went to Colorado for the memorial service. Alex walked to the front of the hall and spoke in a trembling voice to a hundred people, most of them strangers. I'd prepared my own eulogy, but decided not to speak: this was Alex's day to mourn, and my time to be the kind of father who could let her breathe independent of my own needs. If Doug could have seen her up there, he'd have known why I sat silent; I imagined Doug leaning against the post of the corral, laughing out loud, as proud of her as I was.

Chapter Twenty-three:
Ceremony

Leavings

In her junior year of college, Alex left for six months of studying abroad in Italy. When her great grand-parents walked onto the ships that would bring them to this country and down into steerage—rooms were not an option—they were just about her age. They knew that they would never return home, they would never see their parents' faces again except in the photographs they carried and they would never hear their parents' voices again; the first transatlantic telephone cable was a good decade away, and no one in a shtetl would have a telephone anyway. Letters took weeks, maybe a month. In case of an emergency—usually a death, because no matter what happened nothing could be done about it—they would receive a mechanically generated tele-gram.

As we drove to the airport, I realized that the only times Alex and I had not been able to communicate for more than a day or two were when I'd gone on short backpacking trips. Even in Italy, we'd be incommunicado for only the time it would take her to find a Skype connection. I reassured myself that our wired-in world, by making communication more accessible, renders separations less frightening and sorrowful. But although her going to Italy seemed like a pale reflection of her great grandparents' boat rides to America, the feeling of adventure is impervious to any history other than one's own. Only our own perspective tells us that her great-grandparents' trans-Atlantic steerage passage was nothing compared to the journeys of the Vikings and Columbus. Alex's own first merry-go-round solo was Alan Shepard blasting into space, me miles away by the railing as she soared and plunged on her horse, both of us helpless and slightly thrilled.

I remembered when Alex was in middle school, and she'd felt restless and complained that there were no adventures in her life, and not even any prospects for it.. A school orchestra concert, a summer trip somewhere with her mom or me, high school a year away— these, she complained, weren't *adventures*. Finally in her junior year of high school her era of adventures, dormant since the days of perhaps her first walk in the neighborhood alone in the dark, commenced. She went to Italy for a few weeks with her Italian club. Even though she travelled with a group, on her first evening there she phoned me, all excited. She and several of her friends had actually walked out of the hotel without a chaperone, right into the streets of *Rome* and over to a market where she amazed her friends by bargaining with someone, using a skill I'd taught her earlier that year in Tijuana. Her grandfather Herb, who knew how to cut a deal, would have been proud.

It may be that as my grandparents walked onto their boats their emotional circuits quickly blew out. This may explain something about my mother, who wouldn't be born for at least another decade. When I was a child we had a family photo album, bulging with loose pictures of mostly solemn people with stiff clothes and expressions, standing in front of faded backgrounds of places that looked nothing like Chicago. When I was about 17, I decided to look at the album again. My mother finally located it deep in a closet, but to my surprise, at least half the pictures were missing.

"What happened to all the photos?" I asked.

"I threw them out," she said. "All those people are dead."

Once, at the beginning of a hitchhiking trip from Chicago to Seattle, my father drove me about 20 miles out of the city to a decent hitching spot. I knew he didn't want me hitchhiking, that he was afraid for me. Maybe, despite his fears, he felt a little pride or envy too. These were things I now wish we could have talked about, though I would have sidetracked, could not have handled, such a conversation then. Maybe as he drove me to the highway he thought for an irrational moment about taking me all the way across the country. And in fact, because he was retired, there wasn't anything stopping him other than nearly 50 years of marriage, a lifetime of digging the channel in which his own particular life was running, and the fact that we would have been poor traveling companions.

As we checked Alex's baggage at the airport, we talked about inconsequential things. I knew that anything I said even remotely meaningful might bring on tears, hers or mine, and that any last minute advice I had would be more to assuage my own anxiety or to reassure myself that I still had some important role to fulfill. I would rather leave her with nothing at all than have her think of me like old Polonius in *Hamlet*, giving a pompous goodbye speech to his son Laertes. No, I wanted to give her a proper sendoff, to help her walk toward the plane with anticipation and excitement. That seemed like a wise, calculated decision, but in fact family and personal history were roiling inside me in a storm of memory and emotion that smothered anything important I might have thought to say. Denial, sorrow, fear, impotence, embarrassment, pride—the sum total zeroed me out.

We stood there a moment and then it was time for her to turn and, ironically, walk through Security. "Six months is a long time," she said, tremulously. My tears came immediately. I hugged her, pulling her face into my shoulder so she couldn't see my tears, but she either spotted them or felt me shaking.

We both learned something about deflection. "You're crying," she said, her voice muffled into my shoulder.

"No I'm not," I lied. I hugged her tighter until I had my tears under control, and then I said goodbye and let her go, forgetting to tell her that I was so proud of her because she was feeling scared, excited and sad—all the necessary ingredients of adventure.

Ceremony

I was sitting on some rocks on the shores of the Tyrrhenian Sea under a half-moon with Alex, who was nearing the end of her six-month studies abroad, and she asked if I'd like to smoke a joint with her. We'd never smoked together. Instead of telling her the truth, that I'd feel awkward, I said, "Sure." Saying no would have been to insist on maintaining our relationship's 20-year hierarchy, and my visit wasn't about that. She had been showing me around Bologna and Cinqueterre not as a tour guide but as someone in the bloom of living there who felt she knew very well what she was about. She'd ordered for us in restaurants, did all the speaking for us, and this in fact was my main reason for traveling here, to give her the experience of showing off what she'd learned, how much she'd grown. During her six months abroad she'd come a long way since her first week in Bologna, when she'd had to find her own apartment, speaking Italian to do it. The first day in her new apartment, she'd Skyped me from her bedroom, reluctant to walk out into the rest of the apartment and hang with her three new Italian roommates, who'd been living together for about a year. No, this trip, this evening, called for a ceremony to mark her passage.

It seemed like mediocre grass, which was what I'd expected. Fathers, not their kids, can appreciate and afford the difference between quality alcohol and wine coolers, and between knockout and lowgrade dope. I had just taken my third toke when I realized it was powerful creeper. Too late, I declined the fourth.

"This is really powerful grass," I mumbled. I think she smiled; it was difficult to tell because my night vision is just about gone. I looked at the yards of uneven, canted rocks I would eventually have to climb to get back to pavement, figured I could probably do it since I'd gotten out there with only a little trouble, but I knew I'd have to be very, very careful. I didn't want to give my daughter any great stories about how she'd gotten her father stoned and he broke his ankle trying to get back to level ground. Seriously stoned, I kept losing the thread of our conversations or thinking of conversation-ending pieces of advice or sage observations, all of which I had just enough clarity left to squelch. Our silences hung uneasily.

She told me about the time she'd informed her mother, in her sophomore year of high school, that she wanted to go on birth control pills. "Mom really took it calmly," she said. "Then the next day she ambushed me." The ambush occurred at a breakfast place in our neighborhood. "I walked into George's and mom was already sitting in a booth," she said. "She had a briefcase full of pamphlets about birth control, safe sex, and STDs."

"Your mother's always wanted to be the best possible mother she could be," I said, laughing. I wanted to add, "She loves you," but I was dealing with an ambush myself. Surprised, I realized I couldn't say anything more without my voice trembling. Ever since the divorce, I'd often praised Sandy in ways that also carried a slight bite, stressing such things as her good intentions. But sitting on our separate rocks, both of us looking out at the water instead of at each other, listening to the slap of the sea against the rocks, now I felt like I was praising and appreciating Sandy without any trace of condescension or irony. Nearly 15 years after our divorce, something had finally cracked inside me. I felt grateful for tonight's darkness, which hid my eyes.

Suddenly I realized that Alex had reached the

stage where I could finally tell her the story of why I'd survived in the Pecos Wilderness. Although she knew I'd almost died, I'd never told her that I'd decided to live because I'd seen her face floating in the air. But as we often tell ourselves when our courage fails us, the timing didn't seem quite right. Instead I promised myself that sometime during our stay in Italy in the next few days I'd tell her.

The next day over lunch in a small trattoria, in which the owner was also the cook and waiter, I ordered the pasta special. He said, *"Buona scelta,"* obviously pleased, and I thought of the scene in *Lady and the Tramp*, when Tony, the owner-waiter plays *Bella Notte* on his impossibly wide-stretching accordion while Lady and Tramp slowly chew at separate ends of a strand of spaghetti and meet in the middle, hearts dancing and popping in the air. So I finally told her about that moment in the Pecos. But as I told it, I felt myself tamping down the emotion, diluting the tale into anecdote. Although I saw her shiver when I came to the part about seeing her face floating in the high mountain air, I felt slightly embarrassed and unmoved. And so a moment for which I'd waited all those years undramatically slipped past.

Later, we waited for a train in the noon heat. Tired from the day's hiking and the wine, I squatted on my haunches. Then I stood up too quickly and felt myself getting seriously dizzy. "I stood up too quickly," I mumbled, alarmed that the dizziness wasn't subsiding but getting stronger. A wave of drowsiness washed over me, kept coming, a slow tsunami. I knew a wall was somewhere behind me but had no idea whether it was close enough to stop me from falling backwards, whether I'd smash my head against it or miss it entirely. Everything receded; a circle of darkness began to spread, and I had this curious sensation not of sound disappearing but my *awareness* of it disappearing, consciousness dimming. Facing me, Alex noticed me starting to sway side to side, and she put a hand on each of my forearms to steady me. Later I asked whether my eyes had rolled up and back into my head but she said no, they'd just gone blank, which was even more terrifying: this didn't look like a faint to her, but dying. What I remember most is her hands on my forearms, steadying me—her grip a bit tentative, but just strong enough to hold me up.

Chapter Twenty-four:
Pandemic Report

Around March, 2020 during the early days of the pandemic, twenty-year old Alex was halfway across the country from me, worried about her seventy-three year old father who was living on the quickly rising slope of the coronavirus bell curve and still seeing some psychotherapy clients in person. "Relax," I said when she phoned me. "I'm doing fine. You just need to worry about me getting arrested for shooting one of these fucking turkeys who are buying up all the toilet paper."

"You're joking to hide your anxiety," she said, bitching at me. "Stop always joking about things."

"And you're always bitching at me to hide your *own* anxiety," I said. "I'm fine. I wash my hands so often I'm beginning to think I'm a raccoon. I've got wipes in my office. I wipe down doorknobs and light switches, and I don't touch my face."

"Have you told your clients you'll see them on Skype instead of face-to-face?"

"No."

"Why not?"

"Because."

"That's not a good reason," she said.

"You're turning into an old lady nag. You really need to chill. Remember what I've always told you, that I—"

"Don't tell me again that you always laugh at danger."

"But it's true."

"There you go again, joking to hide your feelings."

"I know you're worried," I said, "and I appreciate it. I keep at least six feet between my clients and me, and I don't shake their hands any more, let alone hug them."

"Tell your clients you're going to Skype."

"Sure."

"You're not going to do it, are you?"

"I'll consider it," I said, and on that unsatisfying note we hung up.

When does anxiety disintegrate into paranoia? A month after 9/11 someone started mailing letters dusted with anthrax to newsman Dan Rather and other public figures. Newly feeling vulnerable to attack, Americans got even more nervous. Delores, an elderly woman, proudly told my mother that she was throwing every piece of junk mail she received right down the garbage chute without even opening any of it just in case it had some of that anthrax stuff on it. Did her pride come from outsmarting terrorists or from equating her importance with Dan Rather's? But I also found myself considering whether her garbage chute led directly into an incinerator, which would be a good thing, or into a large bin, which would just be passing the anthrax on to someone else.

Meanwhile the hoarders had loaded up on toilet paper and antiseptic wipes, leaving the grocery shelves bare. Where do we draw our circle of protection: around ourselves, our immediate family, people we know? Do we stretch it wider to include people we don't know? When things get worse, you start to triage with medical care, compassion, and eventually a quick insincere "Sorry," or you stop noticing others at all. Eventually you may even see them as an enemy threatening your own survival. In ordinary times few people would endorse drawing circles of protection that exclude strangers, but in tough times who practices everything they've endorsed? Just like I thought about standing outside Chicago's Trump Tower and trying to shame everyone who walks in or out of there, I wanted to ask the jerks lugging their bales of toilet paper out of stores how they could justify buying so much of it that there was nothing left for anyone else.

At our core we're still primitives huddling close to the campfire, listening to the rustling and the howling in the darkness just beyond. We know the howling of the predator so well because it's also us. So we pray or go to church or play the lottery or hope for recompense for our benevolent thoughts or good deeds, whether from karma or some god, until fear takes over and we toss that kind of thinking out the door and see others as a threat.

Once our ancestors sought refuge from their loneliness and fear by professing that they were a pinnacle of creation or at least that the gods might favor them. After Copernicus took away the comforting notion that we were snugly nested in the center of the universe, Elizabethans still clung to the idea of a clockwork universe vibrating with the music of heavenly spheres. Later, Mendel and Darwin inculcated more doubt into our idea of just who we thought we were and what our rightful place in the universe was. (What kind of monk was that Mendel anyway, announcing the inexorableness of genetics?) After we'd managed to digest the messages of Darwin and Mendel, along came the physicists and astronomers who showed us that not only is Earth just a random mote in the universe, but the entire universe is expanding faster, accelerating away from us. It was as if Little Red Riding Hood had been told that the primeval woods were deeper and darker than she'd even dared to imagine and that there was no grandma's cottage anywhere in there. So why not throw another log on the fire, tote home another multipack of toilet paper?

In the final scene of *Ulzana's Raid*, a 1972 Western which has undeservedly been pretty much forgotten, Burt Lancaster, a mortally wounded grizzled old scout for the U.S. Calvary, is left alone to die on the prairie. Sitting against a rock, he slowly rolls a cigarette, knowing his life will end with this one last smoke. He takes a weary breath, sighs out the word, "shit," and dies. I was 26 when I saw it and thought what a perfect ending, going out with a sigh that blended together weary resignation, bemused regret, and irony. *What's it all been about, and does any of it matter now—this speck of tobacco on my lip, those clouds drifting across the distant mountain peak, memories, everything distilling down into this final moment.* (Unfortunately, in what seems to be the only extant version of the film, the word "shit" has been deleted).

Alex phoned me back five minutes after we hung up. "I'm not going to apologize for anything I said," she said, "but I'm sorry about my tone."

This is the meat of relationships, the capacity of humans to make mistakes and repair, to commit regrettable actions and to atone for them, to keep trying to clear away the detritus and dust that inevitably settles over our connections with each other.

"You're scared for me, I understand that," I said. Just to alleviate my own discomfort, I wanted to keep talking, but my better instincts took over and I chose to stay quiet and keep the connection open instead of fill it with platitudes.

"I've never told you this," she said, "but when I think about whether to have a baby, I can't imagine having a child who didn't know you."

I managed to say I was really touched and that I loved her, and then I shut up again before my voice cracked.

CHAPTER TWENTY-FIVE:
CAPTAIN'S LOG

i

When I was about 10 years old, I read a little pulp book about the Sargasso Sea, a fog-shrouded, silent graveyard for any ship unfortunate enough to have drifted into it. I imagined what it would be like to spend the rest of my life knowing I was trapped, doomed. It felt like a terrible but compelling fate. Years later I learned about the Sargasso Sea's real uniqueness: as the only body of water on our planet without any coastline, the seaweed-choked Sargasso Sea is both finite and without any boundaries except on maps. But maps, just relative guides to our time and place, provide no comfort to the marooned.

I read on Facebook that the daughter of my recently deceased old friend Gordon was going through one of those 20-something crises—a sudden job loss, no emergency bankroll, and rent due in three weeks. I messaged Becca that if she wanted to talk to just let me know. It surprised me that she messaged right back saying yes, can we talk. When Gordon was alive, I'd never filled any useful role for her; Gordon and I had been best friends for over 40 years but always lived half a country apart, and so Becca and I were distant satellites in each other's lives. It had been well over a year since she and I had talked; I'd flown to Buffalo shortly after Gordon learned that he had terminal lung cancer and had less than a year to live.

The three of us had gone out to lunch. Even though she knew he had terminal cancer the conversation was inconsequential—the usual jive we had on those few occasions when we were all together. Gordon and I had been friends for so long that although he hadn't asked me to talk to Becca about his death, I knew this was what he wanted and that he didn't want to be around when the topic came up. So when Gordon went outside for a smoke, I said, "Your dad has a year and a half at most to live. There will be a time or two when he's feeling better and you might get your hopes up, but he's definitely dying. Most people usually wait until the last minute to say what they want to say, and sometimes they wait too late. So you should at least start thinking about what you want to tell him." She nodded and her eyes teared up; usually she never gave anything away, revealed little, except when she was pissed off or impatient. Then Gordon came back and we all relapsed into our usual small talk. He died about eight months later.

After Gordon died, his wife Sue sent me some of his ashes, and I took them down to New Orleans, where I had first met him and where we had both had, if not the best years of our lives, certainly the least responsible, most unfettered and hardest partying ones, sprinkled with mutual consolations and celebrations and awash in a lot of booze, acid, speed, and marijuana, and over a dozen Mardi Gras burning our friendship into our brains. New Orleans is where our twenties and thirties are enshrined. Not believing in any afterlife or that any of us ever owe anything to anyone's memory, I wanted to scatter his ashes to regenerate and to pay tribute to my life as much as his, to try to feel more deeply the fact and the enormity of his loss. I sometimes have an inability to feel the loss of people who are important to me until they're almost gone or gone; I'm usually just missing the train, then running after it and if I'm lucky catching it at the last moment, relieved to have at last made it aboard.

In an effort to feel the loss of someone who had known more different parts of me than anyone else except family, I scattered Gordon's ashes around several of our old haunts. I left some at Bonaparte's Retreat, the gritty bar where we'd first met. Bonaparte's entire north wall had once been covered with a psychedelic mural of a morose, tragic Napoleon standing in the middle of flaming and smoldering ruins. Years ago the owner sold Bonaparte's to someone who turned it into a cheesy souvenir shop, and the new owner nailed wood panels over the mural and then hung shelving. For several years if you peered between the back panel slats you could at least see some of the colors of the mural. Eventually he replaced the panels with sheets of Formica snugged together and then rehung the shelving, so now it's completely hidden. I walked to the north wall of the store and left some of Gordon's ashes on the back of a shelf against the Formica.

Then I walked a few blocks up to Jackson Square. In his homeless days, a few years before I'd met him and the gates to the park had been open all night, Gordon would sleep under the bushes. I had no idea which bushes, so I scattered ashes in various places. Then I left the rest of the ashes in other places around New Orleans where he'd lived. A good 25 years, plus Katrina and gentrification, had wrought changes and so I had to guess about some houses and apartments, even though I'd stayed in them. Time erodes things.

Then I passed the casino. I hate casinos, with the frenzy, the noise, and the same false hopes that religion and notions of an afterlife promise (though at least casinos occasionally deliver the promised payoff). But Gordon had played the lottery every day for his last 20 or 30 years, and I thought, what the hell, I'll go in and play a slot in his memory. I fed a twenty into a machine, already thinking I wanted to be out of there, pressed the Play button and when the symbols stopped spinning I realized that I couldn't even figure out what paid off and what didn't. Pissed off and feeling stupid for being there, I hit the cash out button. Not only didn't I get my change back, but the machine started enticing me to put in more money, shouting, "B-i-i-i-g winner! B-i-i-i-g winner!"

I thought, "Fuck you," and hit the cash out button again and again, wanting to salvage the rest of my twenty and get away from there. Then I noticed that the counter was spinning. Dumbfounded, I watched until it stopped at $865. When I walked outside into the sunlight, I looked up into the sky, shook my head slightly, and smiled, feeling ironic, not spiritual, but still....

ii

Loss is as universal as love. Young birds get nudged out of their nests and kittens, whelps and piglets one day get cuffed away from their mothers' teats. But only human beings fear that the bond will someday end or that we'll eventually die: it's the price we pay for our knowledge of inconstant hearts and mortality. We may tell ourselves that this makes our relationships more complex and richer than the simple ones of animals and babies. But who knows whether that's just a compensatory story to help us deal with our knowledge of death? This kind of complexity helps me make a living as a therapist.

Which comes first, connection or abandonment? If Eden resides in the womb, where we're awash in warm and nourishing amniotic fluid, what about those hurricanes of adrenaline that rage around the fetus when the mother feels fear, or the drying up of nurturing neurotransmitters when the mother's depressed? What does love, abandonment, or loss feel like before we even know the word for it? This interplay of connection and abandonment echoes throughout our lives. When we feel a momentary hint of despair—a cloud drifts across the sun, a darkening thought flickers across our mind, we catch the whiff of a sour memory or death—we reach for the lover, the cigarette, the nachos, the bottle.

iii

Solitude has helped immunize me against loneliness and loss. One birthday, long before the Pecos, I was curious about out of body experiences and thought if it wasn't just nonsense, I might be able to accomplish it on acid in a sensory deprivation tank. After a short while in the tank, I began to get cold and shiver. Because the tank water is heated, I knew the shivering was subjective, and I suddenly thought, "This is how it felt in my mother's womb." Momentarily desolate, I breathed into the cold until I slowly warmed up. Then the dark top of the tank slowly dissolved into a field of stars. My body started shaking again, but not from cold; I was accelerating. The stars moved and blurred, rushing past me, or me rushing past them, like I was traveling at warp speed, and I knew that I was close to leaving my body. Suddenly I thought, what if I can't find my way back? What if out of body experience is just another term for death? Man dies from heart attack in sensory deprivation tank. What if in the next minute I'm looking down from the ceiling of a funeral home at my body in the coffin, people mourning, me soundlessly trying to tell them, "I'm still here!" I deliberately shook and splashed my arms in the water to re-anchor myself.

Once in Kauai I hitchhiked several hours to a dirt path that eventually led to a deserted jungle beach where I pitched my tent and spent my birthday sitting in the sand under a full moon, eating a fresh coconut, the ocean licking the sand, playing an exquisitely melancholy Happy Birthday riff on my harmonica. Even in that loneliness I knew that sharing the evening with anyone would have ruined it.

But there's still the hunger for connecting. Waiting for a train one day I accidentally caught the eye of a schizophrenic man about 20 yards away who was raging at invisible people, swearing and throwing violent punches into the air. Locking onto my eyes, he started toward me, shouting curses and swinging. I didn't want to run and look scared, so when he was just outside arm's range, I met his eyes, held our gaze, and made my voice as gentle as possible. "You're scaring me," I said. He stopped himself the only way he could: he took a huge roundhouse punch, purposely missing me by several inches, and he let the momentum of the punch sweep him down onto the ground. I knelt beside him and asked if he was all right. Dazed by the unexpected connection, he shook his head yes. Kneeling beside him, I offered him a cigarette, and we sat side by side smoking in calm silence until my train came.

Except for the most crazed, desperate, angry people—whether they live in the woods, deserts, mountains or cities—who have only the echo chamber of themselves for company—everyone needs an anchor that bites into the seabed, someone who will listen to them when they say, "I'm here. This is who I am."

Eventually, Gordon married and moved from New Orleans to Buffalo, his new wife's home town. One day I got a call from him. He had just learned from an old New Orleans friend that his ex-wife Dawn was dying of cancer, the first of our cohort to go. Our friend Jane warned him what to expect if he went down there: flailing in the panic that narcissists feel when they're about to lose the most important person in their life, Dawn's husband Ken spent his days brewing foul teas, juices and soups that he was convinced would save her. "Dawn needs her rest," he'd say when someone wanted to come over. He barred the door against friends, doctors, nurses and western medicine—all threats to the miracle he was trying to pull off.

I met Gordon near Memphis, and we drove the six hours to New Orleans. When we were just an hour away I called Ken and told him we were in town and thinking about stopping in, prepared for what he'd say.

"Dawn's not feeling well enough to see anyone today," he said.

"Actually," I replied, "we wanted to see you too. Everyone's so concerned about Dawn that they don't realize how hard this is for *you*. It sounds like you're all alone in this, man. You're doing an incredible job, and you've got to be exhausted. Can we come over and bring something for you?"

Ken said hold on, he'd see whether Dawn was up for

company, and in a moment he returned, said she was feeling a little better today, and we could probably stop by for a little while. When we got there, Gordon took Ken for a walk so I could talk with her. She was lying on a couch, too exhausted to get up.

Dawn's smile, always incandescent, was now only a flicker. I knelt by the couch and squeezed her hand, and she squeezed back weakly. I'd never held her hand before. After a moment, I said, "So, where you at with this?"

Dawn was always so lively that we'd never really looked into each other's eyes without the mania of laughter or acid: a long, slow, intimate connection wasn't in her jitterbuggy personality nor in my shyness. But dying makes new things possible. "Ken's doing everything he can to keep you alive," I said. I gestured the length of her body. "But you're the Captain of your ship, darlin'. Where do *you* want to go with this?"

"I'm tired," she whispered. "I don't think I want to go on." She seemed almost embarrassed to say it.

When Gordon and I traded places, Ken told me in the garden that Dawn just wasn't fighting hard enough, and so he had to do the fighting for both of them. I asked him whether he'd asked Dawn what *she* wanted to do, and the question stopped him cold. It had never occurred to him. When we see an unwanted part of ourselves in someone else, we despise them for it. But eventually I realized that my contempt was just me ignoring something inside myself that I couldn't admit to—the part of me who wished *I* could be overbearing in service of my own wants and needs. Ken didn't want to be alone; he wanted to be loved.

Nearly two decades after Dawn died, I paid Gordon a visit in his own final days. We watched TV and discussed the sort of concrete things death had put on the table. Then he asked what he should say to Becca. I said, "You lazy bastard, for once do your own work." I phoned him a month later, but he was too hazed with morphine to talk. That was it. When Sue phoned and told me it was over, the news had little impact on me. His suffering was over, and I had not yet begun missing him.

But two years after Gordon's death, Becca surprised me by phoning me in the midst of her run of very bad luck, angry about how life sucked, how her boss had treated her, how she was had run out of options.

She didn't say it, probably didn't realize it, but she was missing her father, and I carried the resonance. I assured her that like her father she was a survivor and so she would make it through this too, and that no matter what she did, her life would continue to unfold in unexpected and mostly good ways, because that's how her father's life, surprisingly and often against all odds, had worked out. When we hung up, I surprised myself. I looked up at the sky, said, "Well, Gordon, how did I do?" and I felt both alone and not alone.

iv

Unable to endure staying in his stuffy cabin any longer writing for people who may never see his log the Captain rubs his eyes, blows out his candle, and looks out his smudged windows at the starry canopy of night over the Sargasso Sea. Tired of hearing only his breathing, his footsteps, the scratch of his pen, the Captain steps outside, climbs on top of his cabin roof, and lays on his back looking up at the stars, breathing in the night air and exhaling out into the universe. Occasionally a wave slaps against some other ghost ship, a slowly rotting hull creaks, a wandering breeze whispers into a tattered sail. So many stars, and

at some point in your life you begin to wonder about the
empty spaces between them.

Gradually, the stars in the constellation of my life, those random hotspots—the people that I've known or known of for years—-are dimming and disappearing. My grandmother had a round, deep blue pincushion that fit into my palm, studded with silver pinheads. When I was a child, I'd take out the pins and push them back in, imagining that I was rearranging the universe, as much a god as when I once imprisoned fireflies in a jar, poked holes in the lid, and tossed in a few blades of grass so they could breathe and eat. For a while they glowed inside the jar, my giant face peering in on them, but they soon dimmed and didn't survive through the night.

Physicists—our new augurs—believe that invisible dark matter stitches the stars and the universe together. Missing people doesn't do any good, my mother would say, because they're gone and won't be coming back. But the fear of missing people is inextricably tied in with loving them. I've learned that if you hedge your bets against losing someone, you love less. Underneath my stoicism, love, sorrow and fear always shimmer and glow.

To cope, we fashion our own tales, trying to forget that we're only specks in a universe that we can never fully comprehend. We can't ignore love, sorrow and fear any more than we can stop time; we can only swim in all of it for as long as we can, never knowing for certain whether we're heading somewhere or nowhere. So we write, we love, and in our own time and way we pray, fear, laugh, cry and grieve, each of us trying to find our own particular song, our own way back into connection.

Chapter Twenty-six:
The Home Field

I once envied people like Evel Knievel who roared toward the precipice twisting the throttle wide open to either soar over the abyss or crash in a blaze of adrenaline and glory. I still sometimes think about going after adventure and danger and refusing to adapt or concede to slower reflexes and fears about fragility and incomplete healing. But in the last decade, I've been having a series of Sunrise dreams. We lived together longer than I've lived with any woman other than my mother and sister (of whom I had no say in the matter) or my daughter. I even once risked my life for Sunrise. For a cat.

Because I respected Sunrise's desire for freedom, we trusted each other completely. Each time I moved I tried to find an apartment that could offer Sunrise as much freedom as possible. One place had an enclosed back stairway with a downstairs wood door that required a key to unlock, and I decided to saw a kitty door into it. That way I could leave my second floor apartment open 24/7 so Sunrise could go outside and come home whenever he wanted. Because the absentee landlord was trying to sell the building, I saw no sense taking the risk of asking his permission. My friend Mike came over with a handsaw, a rubber flap and some hardware and had just sawed a small doorway when the downstairs neighbor heard the noise and asked what we were doing. Worried that if I told him the truth he might phone the landlord, I babbled, "This will make the stairway warmer in the winter." Buttressing my explanation with physics, I windmilled my arms and said, "Cold air, warm air." He knew a warmer back stairway was a good thing, so he never called the landlord.

The next apartment—a third floor unit in a courtyard building—impacted Sunrise's freedom in a more difficult way. The front yard of the building had trees and grass, but I couldn't always walk him down the front stairs and then keep checking to see if he wanted back into the building, so I'd let him out the back door onto the porch, where he'd go down into a labyrinth of stairways and dirty gangways that all led to an alley. I consulted with Mike about constructing a cat-sized winch elevator off my tiny front balcony, but after giving the idea more consideration than it merited, Mike explained that to keep the ascent and descent of the crude elevator from banging into the building or snagging on a lower balcony, the arm holding the pulley would have to be several yards long, and that didn't even take into account jerry-rigging some kind of buzzer system with a pressure sensitive switch on the floor of the cage so I'd know when to haul Sunrise up.

One freezing winter night I heard Sunrise calling plaintively in the back. He'd gotten onto the roof of the building next door: workers had left a ladder on my porch which led up to the roof of the building across the gangway, and somehow he'd crawled up there. It was a treacherous climb, not just for Sunrise but, even worse, for me. The rungs were coated and bearded with ice, and between my porch and the roof the ladder stretched about twenty feet over a three-story drop. I was also drunk.

Muttering miserably, I took off one glove—I would need a bare hand to grab Sunrise when I got within range—and I clutched the first icy rung, trying to take a few deep breaths in the ten below zero air. He stood on the edge of the roof, patiently waiting. My desperate plan entailed getting within reach of Sunrise, acting calm so as to not alarm him, reaching out and scratching his head, and then grabbing him by the nape of his neck and holding him away from my face over the abyss because he'd start clawing frantically the minute I grabbed him, all the while wrapping my free arm tightly around the ladder, clutching for dear life, and making my way back down as fast as I safely could until I was close enough to my porch to fling him backwards. It seemed too much to successfully handle, but there was nothing else to do.

When I got close enough to the edge of the roof, I muttered soothing words to Sunrise that I didn't believe—this was years before I became a parent and perfected this act—then shot my hand out, grabbed him and made my way back down. When I rejoined Sunrise on the porch, I opened the back door so he could run inside and warm up. Instead of immediately following him, I sank to my knees on the freezing porch saying, "Fuck, fuck, fuck."

About ten minutes later, Sunrise wanted out again and of course I let him go. Soon I heard him crying, went out on the porch, and there he was *again*, up on the roof. It was the only time in our years together that I questioned his intelligence. "You got up there," I muttered, "you can get back down," and I went back inside. Sure enough, he eventually showed up at our door.

Another apartment, an illegally converted attic, had a terminally neglected backyard of waist-high weeds in which Sunrise spent his days prowling like a lion in the jungle and ambushing mice, birds and other cats. There were no stairs to my rickety back porch, so I could leave my back door wedged open all day and night and Sunrise, whenever he wanted food or warmth or company, could climb the drainpipe and come inside to eat, sleep with me, or hunt cockroaches. The miserable apartment was good enough for me and an ideal arrangement for Sunrise.

ii

From my mid-20's until early into my 40's when I hitchhiked around the country and backpacked, like Sunrise I kept moving toward freedom. When I was approaching 40 and about to propose to Sandy, I went to New Orleans on what became my last hitchhiking trip. It felt important to keep hitching, a way to prove to myself that love and marriage didn't mean embracing a more stale kind of hitch. Just after twilight in central Illinois, a beat-up car stopped ahead of me. I trotted to meet him and as I neared I saw four guys sitting in it wearing dirty shirts. Before I got in, they asked me if I had money for gas, and I gave my standard heading off trouble line: "Hell, if I had any money I wouldn't be hitching." They drove off without letting me in, and suddenly I thought, "They could have stolen whatever I had and shot me while I stood by their car. You can die that easy, that quick." I'd always known that, but this time I *knew* it.

I made it into New Orleans late the next night—my twelfth Mardi Gras. With a woman I loved waiting for me back home, I felt freed from the hunt for love or sex that could sometimes turn Mardi Gras into lonely work, and I wandered content through the revelry, shadowed only occasionally by the thought of the long hitchhike home into the winter. On the hitch back toward Chicago, south of Memphis it began to rain and it didn't let up. Two hours later, I was stuck in a noisy, ugly spaghetti junction still on the outskirts of

Memphis, the temperature had dropped to 35 degrees, and the rain had changed to sleet. I walked off the highway, took a cab to the airport and bought a ticket home. At the Memphis airport counter, I listened to the agent's southern accent and felt sad, wondering whether I'd ever hear a southern accent again.

A year later, after my marriage and shortly before Alex was born, something went terribly wrong with Sunrise. In his final week, he went out only twice and crawled immediately under the bushes against the house. Fresh air and freedom didn't give him any pleasure; he went outside only out of habit, compulsion. When I was certain that he would never recover, and I believed that his suffering overwhelmed any excitement, peace or pleasure he could ever again find, I phoned the vet and asked him to come to our house with his bag. I held Sunrise as he relaxed into death, and I thought with surprising relief, "Going to sleep's not just a euphemism." It was about five years later, after Alex was born, that I had my own bout with dying in the Pecos.

In my dreams about Sunrise, I'm always looking for him; he's been missing for some time, but I always find him. In my most recent dream, something new happened. I'm climbing along the side of a huge sand dune, and Lynn, her voice muffled by the distance, calls to me saying she's located him. I make my way back, and when I get there I see Sunrise sleeping soundly on a porch, snuggled against another cat. The building is some kind of institution, and he looks great—clean, well fed, relaxed, so comfortable, so well-taken care of that I feel both relieved and sad. I can't decide what to do, what's best, what's right. If I wake him, call to him, I know he'll recognize me and come back home with me to a less comfortable but more extemporaneous life. Or I can silently walk away for good, without him knowing I'd been there, leaving him to live out the rest of his days in safety and comfort.

In the particular way that dreams roll together events and themes of your life, the dreamscape sand dunes resonated with the first time I saw *Lawrence of Arabia* and was swept away by the beautiful, harsh landscape and by Lawrence, that solitary man who couldn't abide the conventions of the life he'd been born into. Lawrence walking alone through the immensity of the dunes, compulsively seeking adventure. I felt thrilled, even though I knew that his glorious trek would become a slog toward tragedy. And something else about that dreamscape hill. Six years after Sunrise had died, in my sixth year of my marriage that would not last beyond seven, when I'd gotten so lost in the Pecos Wilderness, at some point I'd desperately staggered halfway up a rugged hill and tried to walk along it, hoping that I might see the way out or that someone might miraculously spot me.

Twice in the next few years after the Pecos I tried backpacking again, but my aging Midwestern body could no longer function well enough in the mountain air to carry a backpack into the high solitude, and I had to leave the mountain wildernesses for good. Several years later, when I was in my 60's and living safely in the city, I slipped on some black ice and had my smashed ankle rebuilt with screws and a plate—a long, slow, incomplete rehab. Now in winter when I see anything on the sidewalk that even *looks* like it might be icy, I literally feel my foot slide on it. Sometimes as a reality check, I'll stop, stand firmly, re-step on the spot with one foot, and discover that it's not icy at all. Some questions never have clean answers.

I still occasionally miss the days of hitchhiking and backpacking, but the fact that I did them has gradually come to matter more than the loss of them. As for the former hormonal hurricanes of love, I've found that love works best when it's savored rather than devoured, when it's held easily rather than clutched. Loving well in my 70's, I've learned, results from years of luck, good and bad, and from having acquired enough skills at this sort of thing to keep it going. It's not about trying to transcend or obliterate loneliness but about choosing to love someone the best we can in the shadows of mortality.

PART FOUR:
WALKING INTO CLIMATE CHANGE

Living Well
While the Hourglass Trickles

*K*nowing that everything eventually ends doesn't necessarily help us accept our mortality with equanimity. Sometimes it does seem to motivate us, though, to clutch at life more fervently or run from death more desperately. Most of our strategies sure beat sitting in a death row cell just watching the clock. Hummingbirds and bees know how to live: while they're flitting and buzzing around gathering nectar, they don't worry about the nectar running out. They just go on gathering.

CHAPTER TWENTY-SEVEN:
AT THE MOVIES

Movies have always been my great pleasure and escape. But I saw two movie trailers in a row a few years ago where the cutting, the music, the chanting chorus and the narrative urgency crescendoed and accelerated until my heart was pounding at the prospect of a movie I knew I never wanted to see even while I couldn't turn my eyes away from the screen. When I was a kid and Cinemascope and Technicolor were new, they still had curtains in front of the screen, and as the triumphant music began, and the 20th Century Fox spotlights or the roaring MGM lion or Miss Columbia undulated wavy behind the curtains and the curtains slowly parted, my only anxiety was whether the curtains would get completely opened before the movie began. I still see the curtains opening on the Lone Ranger, on a rearing Silver, framed against a cerulean sky. That Lone Ranger movie was my first date, in about sixth grade. I stretched my arm and rested my hand on the far shoulder of Sheri and told myself that every time the camera shot changed I would inch my arm a little further down toward her breast. It took so long that before my arm was halfway there my hand fell asleep and I had to remove my arm entirely and go back to digging in my popcorn box.

Both excitement and anxiety make our hearts pound and our pulses accelerate: sometimes the zeitgeist is charged with one, sometimes the other. The first time I saw *2001: A Space Odyssey*—in Cinerama, in the 1960's, sitting in the front row of the balcony with my new and first college girlfriend—as the man ape magnificently pounded with his bone and then flung it soaring in slow motion end over end into the sky while the triumphant *Thus Spake Zarathrustra* blared, I couldn't help it, I turned to Eva, she turned to me, and we smiled, thrilled. Eva and I, simultaneously swept away by something greater than ourselves, wanted nothing from each other in that moment except to share it.

Movies both reflect and amplify the zeitgeist. Captive, I watched the horror movie trailers, telling myself I wouldn't see these movies, I don't need more anxiety. I thought what the world needs instead is a calm movie, maybe even call it *Calm Movie,* the opening shot a straight-on close up of a giant benevolent face filling the screen—the Dalai Lama would be good—

smiling right at you, just smiling, and maybe after a half minute, a long time in movie time, he slowly raises his hands, puts his palms together, silently blesses you and the entire audience. But then my anxiety washed back in and I thought, how many people would actually go see a movie like that with a long nothing-happening opening? It would need to pretty quickly develop a narrative hook, and as the inexorable chorus of demonic voices in the horror psychopath trailer picked up steam, I thought there's no sense even thinking about what the hook might be, because where would I get the money to do this project anyway, how could I possibly do a movie when I'm already past 70, prematurely drawing down my retirement fund, and the cancer's probably going to come back in a few years? Doesn't that timing suck, I thought: I'll be sick just when climate change turns our society into dog-eat-dog survival of the fittest, and what's going to happen to my daughter?

Calm Movie, I thought, definitely *Calm Movie* is needed. A lot of nature shots, slow dissolves, and soothing music. Years ago I saw a documentary with polar bears swimming under blue Arctic skies, and I remember thinking life is good for all of us: a leisurely dip and abundant food everywhere, from poolside bars in tropical resorts where the weather was hot but not brutal—merely as hot as it was ever going to get—to cruises among the fjords to see the glaciers that we assumed would still be there for our grandchildren. Last night on TV I saw another clip of polar bears, now swimming for their lives, looking desperately for a patch of ice large enough to rest on. The second horror movie trailer was about a murderous hitchhiker.

"What do you want!?" screamed the bloodied victim.

"Just say four words," said the psychopath, who appeared to be the only calm one in the movie: "I… want…to…die." Endgame, checkmate, the Grim Reaper marching into the new millennium.

Maybe *Calm Movie* could get away with a thesis instead of a plot. Calm begets calm might be a good one. The Dalai Lama, sitting in a lotus position, spreads his palms, turns into a giant flower. But now the petals part like curtains, revealing a stamen, bright red, which grows, then swells into Satan's erection, a red hot mushroom pouring down heat over the world.

In the movie theaters today, vibrating with anxiety, we gnaw on our knuckles like they're popcorn until we start to devour ourselves.

Chapter Twenty-eight:
Love and Climate Change

Even as I neared 60, I still believed that I could keep readjusting, cheating, or denying my mortal time clock for a while. I could say that my cancer was cured and gone. I could still move the chronological markers between middle and old age downfield a bit. I watched my muscles as I worked the weight machines, and I thought, "That part of my body looks pretty damn good."

But concern about my own death had almost completed its migration from my psyche's constellation of fear into its constellation of knowledge, and larger things than thoughts about my dying began recalibrating my internal clock. I'd gradually become fearful that we were moving toward the extinction of species, including our own, which made the nuances of resetting my clock more complex. Mass extinction and the end of civilization wouldn't have bothered me as much, I thought, if I didn't have a daughter in her final year of high school. Because of Alex, I tried to imagine, like the desert island castaway who puts messages into bottles and throws them into the sea, that each item I pitched into the recycling bin might help insure her rescue.

Doom is never a popular topic. A few weeks before our kids' graduation, we parents threw a little high school graduation party for them. Standing on the deck of the top floor of a high-rise, looking at Chicago's skyline, another father and I talked pleasantly for a long time, laughing and sharing thoughts about our girls, his youngest and my only child, leaving for college in a few weeks. In the past forty years, the skyline had changed so much that my younger self wouldn't have recognized it. I remembered a beacon on top of the Palmolive Building (before it became the Playboy building, before it became something else), sweeping the skyline, letting the lazily buzzing propeller airplanes know that O'Hare was nearby and helping them avoid hitting the Prudential, the tallest building in Chicago. That evening I couldn't even see the Prudential from the deck: too many taller buildings now blocked it out, and the Palmolive beacon had been shut off years ago when the residents living in the lower midriff of the newly built Hancock Center complained that it was shining right into their living rooms.

The father told me he was thinking about moving to Phoenix in about a year. I mentioned that I'd just come from a visit to Phoenix and that as I drove through the city shimmering in its 20th consecutive day of near or above 105 degrees, it had struck me that Phoenix had grown to where it's just about unsustainable and was about to move to the next phase of fulfilling its name.

"If you're thinking long term, I suppose it does make more sense to stay here where there's plenty of water," he conceded. I said, "For *now* there's plenty of water," laughing to keep the conversation light but thinking that even the Great Lakes weren't immune from the escalating demands from further away towns to start piping water. Lakes Meade and Powell wouldn't last nearly as long: they were already projected to disappear in about 25 years. The giant underground Ogallala aquifer, responsible for turning the Great Plains into the nation's breadbasket, was dropping fast, and parts of the once mighty Colorado River already looked more like the Colorado Drainage Ditch. But he was still moving out to Arizona. The changes he didn't want to admit were always just beyond the horizon. I didn't say any of this; I've learned not to argue with anyone about religion, politics or the environment.

But even though I laughed when I said, "For now there's plenty of water," his face changed. "You're not believing that global warming crap, are you?" he said, and he meant it. An intelligent and well-read man, he was nevertheless sick and tired of being besieged by all this media garbage that kept slapping against the shoreline of his comfort like raw sewage on our beaches. An architect, he went to church regularly, put all his tools neatly away each time even when he was in the middle of a project, and his closets, I suspected, were perfectly in order. Global warming didn't fit into his schema of how things are supposed to work out. Why bother reminding people that we've been living on environmental credit even before prospectors tore up the Black Hills and we shot thousands of buffalo from the railroad cars and left them to rot on the prairies? We learned environmental stewardship from the conquistadores.

Even though I turned our conversation back to safe and pleasant things, he decided to go inside and check out the buffet table, and barely ten minutes later he left the party. I wondered whether I'd accidentally forced him to divert too much energy into denial, which didn't leave him enough firepower for pleasantries. Not that I don't do plenty of denial myself. Alex was going off to college, a great adventure for her, entering the halfway house between adolescence and adulthood, and although I was excited about the next segment of her life, I'd begun to worry about the quality of her life forty years from tonight. In 1964, when I was 18, we didn't worry about survival; instead, we believed we would change the world for the better, and whether the world conformed to our wishes and demands or not, we still figured *we'd* be okay.

What, I wondered, were my responsibilities as a parent to try to prepare Alex for the coming decades? Making her anxious wouldn't help. Should I give Alex hope and continue pointing her toward a mirage, encourage her to take as many courses in as broad a range as possible, to open her mind, ears, eyes, and heart to the best that's been written, sung, painted, and said, to the greatest thoughts and discoveries of human beings reverberating around her? Would that help her cope with our species devolving toward its end? Or should I help prepare her for the real future and instead of giving her a violin to fiddle, maybe I should advise her to scrap college, take martial arts classes and go live with our well-armed friends in rural Colorado who would hold their own against savage marauders? The week before, she and her friends had organized a neighborhood scavenger hunt. They came back laughing with their stash of magazine covers, plastic bags with store logos from the local supermarket, and digital photo proof that their team had piled into a shopping cart in its parking lot. They couldn't imagine a scavenger hunt where they'd dig through garbage bins for food, fighting off others.

To awaken more people to the dangers lying ahead, some people talk, write and sing about the beauty of our planet and nature. Their premise is that if you love something enough, you'll take whatever actions are necessary to save it. But that alone doesn't work with deteriorating relationships or with climate change. Unless we acknowledge the awful reality of the loss that's already beginning to unfold, songs of love can become just a romantic bromide. I'd learned some things about love and loss myself living with Alex. When she was in middle school and her boyfriend broke up with her, I had never heard her cry like that:

a desolate, hopeless keening that left me helpless and remembering a despairing lesson I'd learned during her colicky baby days: sometimes the only thing others can do for your pain is to feel bad about it.

"Do you think the time you'd had with Nate is worth the sadness you're feeling now?" I'd asked. She decided that yes, it was.

So she began to learn about the fundamental equation of human beings, from junkies to star-crossed lovers to victims of terrible accidents and diseases: weigh the suffering against the pleasure, and divide by time. In the Egyptian Book of the Dead, Annubis weighs the heart of the deceased against the feather of Maat, the goddess of truth, justice and harmony. If the heart is lighter or weighs the same as the feather, the deceased can proceed to the afterlife. If the heart is heavier, Ammut, the fierce crocodile/ panther/ hippopotamus, devours it. But although I'd given Alex some balm for her wounds, I knew that she'd learn only by experience. We try to learn vicariously—that's one reason why people swap stories, read literature and watch movies—but more often than not, we learn by falling or crashing, by getting burned and cut, and then rescued, soothed and healed.

Loss. Now my daughter was heading off to college, sailing into years of continuing heartbreaks, loves, pains, revelries, hangovers, hopes, uncertainties, revelations, exhilarations and ennui, only now I'd see almost none of it as it happened, would know it only through the emotional and chronological disjunction of narrative—and then only some of it, like looking down from a jetliner at a small boat in the middle of the ocean.

As assuredly as we're born to die, we procreate to eventually let go. The gift and paradox of parenting is that every day you know the importance of your child to you while always keeping in mind that you can't, mustn't think about holding on. Attraction and pulling apart, holding on and letting go are built into the atoms of our lives. Exquisite musical notes die their haunting deaths. Life's a simultaneous ache and glow; the do-si-do of pain and pleasure; the itch of the healing wound; the revolving door of spring and fall that quickens as you age. Words like shalom, salaam, caio and aloha and the tearful hug mean both hello and goodbye. We raise our children and hold on to them, our time together seasoned by the knowing that we need to prepare to let go.

I thought maybe I needed to remind Alex—and myself—what I'd been learning that was as powerful as my knowledge of doom: if you imbue and invest as many individual moments as you can with quality, compassion, enthusiasm, and love then *ipso facto* you live well, have beat the odds, and you will depart, whether today, tomorrow or in a few decades, knowing your life has been worthwhile and a good one. Breathe on each ember, even though you know that each ember will always turn to ash.

In his essay "The Hanging" Orwell's handcuffed prisoner, walking toward the gallows, steps around a muddy puddle in the road. Already condemned and miserable, he still didn't want to get his feet wet. And what if he'd paused an extra moment to look at the ripples in the muddy puddle, watch an ant scurrying along its edges, wondered whether the weeds subtly waving at the side of the road felt on some cellular level their own swaying? What if he'd looked at the muddy reflection of the sky in the puddle and then thought to lift his eyes to the panoramic sky itself? The person who lives well, who learns and loves, as well as the fretters, the avaricious, and the brooders, will all die.

The winners don't survive the longest; the winners live the best. It doesn't matter for whom the bell tolls, the nightingale sings, or the oceans sough and roar. As long as you can hear them, they, and you, have mattered.

Chapter Twenty-nine:
Hamstrung

At the beginning of my near-disaster in the Pecos, I'd lost the trail and found myself deep in a low-lying forest. I knew I should backtrack and try to pick up the trail where I'd lost it, but anxiety had already started to eat away at my decision-making, so I decided to just push on ahead and try to find the trail again on the other side of the woods. Fortunately I took only about forty more steps before realizing that if I kept going I could get even more lost and never be able to backtrack. Maybe I had already gone too far. Which way *was* the way back? I forced myself to stop, sit on a fallen tree, and take deep breaths for several minutes. Then I backtracked and managed to pick up the trail. (Much, much later in the day I lost it again, this time irrevocably, but at least I didn't lose it out of panic). Eventually I always manage to rescue myself from anxiety and despair with my own brand of timorous optimism. Temperamentally, I usually can't just rush ahead. But I can't just keep sitting still forever hoping something will happen either: *that's* the gateway to depression.

As a child I saw a *Flash Gordon* episode in which Flash was locked in a room with two walls that kept inching closer and closer together. (What the hell kind of a name was Flash Gordon? Generic American, I suppose, unlike Ming the Merciless). In an early childhood exercise contemplating mortality, I tried to imagine my last minutes in that room of doom. Would I lie parallel to the floor, pressing my hands against one wall and my feet against the other, straining futilely to stop the walls? When that didn't work and I realized that my leg bones were starting to push into my hips, I'd stand absolutely straight, holding my breath and facing an encroaching wall to make myself thinner. Would I face it or turn my back to it? Years later, I thought about the person who'd have to clean me off the walls: no matter how bad things are, somebody's always got it worse. Like my mother used to tell us on budget-saving dairy night when she made her greasy salmon patties, children are starving in Africa.

I'm so lousy at anxiety that I can't succeed at letting it dominate me for long. Eventually I pep talk myself into thinking that some solution might glimmer ahead. But I often strive with as much irony and sarcasm as hope. Mark Twain said he didn't want to go to heaven because of the kind of people who'd be there, and I might stop from moving ahead too quickly by fearing that when I came into the sunlight a chorus of Pollyannas or religious people telling me God had saved me would be holding a welcome party.

Once, Lynn persuaded me to go on a candyass vacation to Palm Springs—my mountain backpacking days were well in the past. "We can hike in Joshua Tree," she said. Not a rugged adventure, but a taste of nature, a chance to avoid an argument with Lynn, and a break from city life. Wouldn't you know it though, a week before we left, our airplane tickets and Airbnb nonrefundably paid for, I pulled a hamstring. The hiking was to be my main pleasure of the trip: as long as I can move, I feel better. That's why quicksand always seemed like such a horrible ending. I once learned that if you get stuck in quicksand struggling accelerates the sinking, so you should lie on your back. But lie on your back so that what? You sink more slowly? What are the odds that someone will be walking through the swamp, see you there and throw you a rope? Why would they be in a swamp in the first place, and would they even *have* a rope? The only good thing about dying in quicksand is that no alligators are coming at you.

Movement has always promised me some measure of safety and relief. As a child I learned about the Sioux warriors' Sundance. Their entire way of life irrevocably quashed, Sundancing became their excruciating expression of hope, a torturous dance for freedom, a Good Friday without a surrogate Christ doing their suffering *for* them. They drove a piece of wood through their pecs, tied one end of a long rawhide thong to the wood and tied the other end tautly to a tall pole, and they danced around the pole, hoping to summon better days.

Moving and keeping on keeping on keeps me in the game. "Why not use some walking poles?" Lynn suggested.

"And next month maybe I can hire someone to change my fucking diapers," I silently responded.

About a mile into the Joshua Tree hike, my hamstring started aching pretty badly. I began to worry that I might tear it worse, and at my age the odds of coming out of surgery and making a full recovery are pretty slim. "As good as new" is a promise made only to younger people. What if I kept walking and went so far that I couldn't get back, maybe had to start crawling, doing two miles on my hands and knees on hard packed dirt and sand and sharp stones? But I didn't stop. I adapted. I started stepping with the good leg and bringing my injured leg even with it, minimizing the stretch on the hamstring. But if I was going to look like an old crippled guy, I decided I may as well, God help me, use the walking poles. The slower pace helped me remember what's important about hiking, whether in the mountains or someday around the block from the nursing home: taking the time to see, to listen, to sniff, to spot the skittering little lizard, the small bird perched so lightly on a delicate sprig that it's riding it, a hawk cruising past a distant mountain. Sniffing the difference between wild sage and creosote, pondering whether that distant soft rushing noise is a canyon wind or a dry creek coming to life in the spring melt.

CHAPTER THIRTY:
HOPE AT THE EDGE

i

After my near fatal trip into New Mexico's Pecos Wilderness, I didn't go into the mountains again for about two years. But then I began desperately missing something in the high wilderness that I couldn't find anywhere else—solitude, complete freedom from demands and constraints of people and of everyday life, and a pride in being able to experience what no one else in my life knew about: hiking steadily uphill for hours with a full backpack, testing my strength and stamina, and finally getting high enough to where the lines on the topographic map gave way to mountain lakes and high pastures, scat replaced dogshit, and the only sounds I could hear were my own and the natural world's. Finding somewhere where I could pitch my tent in an spot with a vista of mountains and a quiet, lonely lake and then spend three or four days with nothing I needed to do but occasionally fill my canteen, collect branches and twigs so I could cook a simple meal, and listen to the occasional birdcalls and random breezes that wandered through the passes and across the grassy high pastures. Hearing a far off grumble of thunder and having the time and the long view to track whether the storm would eventually chase me into my tent or drift past a mile or two away while I lay in a sunlit meadow watching distant lightning flashes and columns of dark rain.

Then, at fifty years old and Alex away at college, I returned to Colorado's Raweh Wilderness, my familiar backpacking area. After several hours of uphill hiking, I was just about twenty minutes short of the pristine, secluded lakes and pastures at timberline when the trail came to a single log stretching about twenty feet across and twenty feet above a rushing river. I tightened my backpack to make sure it wouldn't slide on my back and throw me off balance and I crawled on the log to the other side. But the noise of the river put me back in the Pecos, when I'd slipped in the rapids, suddenly found myself in water up to my chest, nearly got swept away, lost my gear, and my trip had taken that steep turn toward disaster. The experience must have remained inside me like a retrovirus; now two years later, when I reached the other side of the log, I stayed on my hands and knees, breathing heavy, trying to calm down. A terrible presentiment took hold that I was going to die on this backpacking trip. I tried to reassure myself that this was merely a long-deferred traumatic reaction, fear reaching out from the past and pressing on the nape of my neck.

Finally I stood and began the last easy uphill leg of the trail, home free. Almost immediately I saw a scarred, dead tree, recently cleaved and seared by lightning, so stark that it seemed a signpost, a warning of death. I stood several minutes, telling myself that I was being irrational, that it made more sense to continue just an easy third of a mile more to where the mountain leveled out into the high pastures and lakes above timberline and I could set up camp, spend a few days finding my rhythm in nature, and then catch another trail down so I wouldn't have to go over that log again. But I kept staring at the signpost tree and finally I told myself that if I continued, whether my terror was PTSD or an accurate premonition, I would be scared every moment I camped, completely alone in the wilderness wrestling with fears of lightning, rattlesnakes, UFOs, a psychopathic murderer, a heart attack, and that I had nothing to prove to anyone, including myself, by continuing this trip. So I turned around, crawled back over the log, and five hours later checked into a motel.

I tried once more two years after that and couldn't make it even close to timberline, in a candyass state park where families with children day tripped. My aging Midwestern body could no longer adjust to the low oxygen at higher elevations. A new physical limit, not fear, stopped me. How does each of us cope with grieving—for parts of ourselves and for the other losses, both sudden and anticipated, that inevitably accumulate?

ii

Nearly 20 years after the Pecos, after Alex had graduated college and was launched, Lynn and I went to the Caribbean island of Grenada for tamer, more comfortable pleasures, the kind of vacation I disdained in my backpacking days. Her friend Mike, his 26-year old son Dave, and I were going to hike to the top of Mt. Qua Qua, a paltry 2,000 feet. Near the trailhead, a badly weathered sign reminded us that everyone has the power to do something about the thinning ozone layer, dating back to when people talked about thinning ozone instead of climate change. For a brief moment, I recalled a scene from a post-apocalyptic movie in which a weathered, broken entrance sign to a deserted amusement park clattered in the wind. The sign reminded me of the broken statue in Shelley's *Ozymandias*:

...Two vast and trunkless legs of stone
Stand in the desert. Near them, on the sand,
Half sunk, a shattered visage lies, whose frown
And wrinkled lip and sneer of cold command
Tell that its sculptor well those passions read . . .
[O]n the pedestal these words appear —
"My name is Ozymandias, king of kings:
Look on my works, ye Mighty, and despair!"
Nothing beside remains. Round the decay
Of that colossal wreck, boundless and bare
The lone and level sands stretch far away.

Instead of Ozymandias' cruel, arrogant hope, my own brand of hope is tender, sad, desperate, fearful. But whatever its flavor, hope helps us cope with the meaningless of life, the randomness of events, and the inevitability of death. Sometimes, however, hope fuels denial, gets in the way of taking action. When the bad guy comes toward Stan Laurel, Stanley puts his hands over his own eyes, hoping the bad guy won't see him. Welcome to climate change.

I've often lived with a combination of hope and anxiety, heavier on the anxiety. But because I almost died, I know in a way I couldn't have known before that someday, unless I get suddenly cheated by a massive heart attack or drunk driver, I'll reach that point again when I'm ready to meet my death. This helps give me the anxious man's immunity: whether I'm mugged or one day find myself face to face with the Grim Reaper, I will feel better if I can say to my assailant, "I knew you were coming." I want my most implacable enemies to know that I'm no fool, even if they don't give a damn *what* I think.

The Pecos, and my later rendezvous with prostate cancer, reminded me to appreciate good moments even more. I still like to empty my mind and watch cumulus clouds. I still light up when I hear kids laugh, thrill when the theater lights dim and the movie begins. I still like drinking wine slowly, and when I smoke good dope I smoke just enough to ride the high rather than smoke too much and weigh myself down into lethargy. I write.

As Mike, Dave and I walked past the ozone layer sign at the Qua Qua trailhead, I thought that even when it was new, its hopeful message was true only in the most general, useless sense. The people of Grenada never had any power to save the ozone layer, just as they can do nothing about climate change. The hurricane belt will continue to expand and eventually embrace Grenada, and the rising seawaters will spill over St. George. Many Grenadians were already talking about shifts in the seasons and winds. (Climate change is more unfair to the island nations, who have done less to cause it than the largest and richest nations but will be affected earlier by it. I remember a tour guide at Chichen-Itza explaining that the kings' houses were always at the heads of the rivers that flowed through the towns, so they had the cleanest water while everyone else used the water that the royal families had washed and defecated in).

Less than half-way up the trail toward the top of Qua Qua, carrying a day pack with just two bottles of water, I was surprised and disappointed at how quickly I got winded and slightly dizzy. Sure, the trail was steep, muddy and slippery, but 2,000 feet was nothing, and I'd been working out for a year building up my muscles and cardio-vascular. Ego began battling with fear. I hated being in last place, the drag on the expedition, watching my friends get further and further away from me and knowing that around some bend they were having to wait for the old guy to catch up. But my heart was pounding hard, and I knew not to try walking through it, so I adopted a regimen of twenty steps, twenty seconds' rest, and then another twenty steps. The sharply canted, slippery trail kept sliding me toward the edges of ravines, and my calves and thighs grew weaker against the pull off the trail. But I kept going, mostly because *not* continuing would have brought on too much self-loathing and regret. I wouldn't quit until the price got higher.

So I found myself in my familiar approximation of full tilt living: struggling in the swirls of striving and pain, pride and fear. As the gap between my friends and me widened, I started forcing myself to count more slowly during the rests and then make sure that I didn't start rushing the next twenty steps. I kept trying not to care about Mike and Dave getting further and further up the trail. These are the kind of adjustments we learn as we get past middle age; we learn that ego is the cheese in death's mousetrap. Compensating for lost time instead of using up some of my steps avoiding the muddiest parts of the trail, I slogged straight through the mud. We didn't bring enough water, so I tried to drink not when I felt thirsty or slightly dizzy but only in the spots where there was a greater possibility of mis-stepping, crashing down into a ravine and having to wait several hours until my friends could fetch a rescue team: I didn't want to be lying down in the brush and mud desperately wishing I'd taken that last drink of water. I savored each sip, washed it around in my mouth before I swallowed.

This capacity for pure appreciation, which we had as babies and then lose in floods of hormones and ego, can grow stronger again as we age. During my twenty-second respites I mused about what psychological actuarial table measures the ignorance of youth and the recklessness of adolescence against the fragility of aging. I remembered Scratch, one of the loosest people I ever knew in New Orleans: he'd walk to the edge of the pool table and in one quick motion bend and shoot and almost always make his shot. But whenever he took time to carefully line the shot up, he'd blow it. We were 23 then, and his unconcern about everything seemed to me the way to live; on the other hand, before he reached 30 he'd burned out his brain with acid and speed. My concentration started drifting; *watch where you're going*, I reminded myself: *most disasters come from not paying sufficient attention.* I tried to say this to myself in a way that sounded wise, not nagging.

iii

When we finally reached the top of Qua Qua, a chilly wind blew constantly—the same trade wind that in terms of what geologists call deep time carried Columbus across the ocean less than an hour ago. Many people believed that Columbus would sail to the edge of the ocean and drop off the edge of the planet. Others believed he would sail into the maws of giant sea monsters looming beyond the horizon. Each generation finds its own dreads, but we may be the first to lack enough of a sense of wonder to compensate for them.

I used to believe that progress and hope were

intertwined and leading toward some better purpose. But increasingly it seems to me that progress comes at a price. We live longer lives with no greater appreciation of them. Automobiles, airplanes, telephones, the Internet have expanded our horizons and built elasticity into our relationships, but whatever's more accessible is usually less valuable: Bali isn't really Bali anymore, and aren't your conversations with Aunt Esther a thousand miles away in her gated community pretty much the same script, even with Zoom? I remember a piece on our local news decades ago about an amazing new store, Blockbusters, where you could actually rent videotapes of all the movies from your past. But now every time I see a movie, I no longer accumulate new memories or relive old ones of where I'd seen it the other times in my life, with whom, and what had been going on for me. The other day I took an old copy of Kazanzatkis's *The Last Temptation of Christ* from my bookshelf, noticed British spellings and suddenly remembered that I'd bought the book in Thessaloniki when I was 24 years old and in the middle of six months hitchhiking through Europe with Cheryl. Surprised, I saw handwriting in the margins that was no longer mine, like fossils in shale. Kindle won't do that for us. The Internet has put previously unimaginable amounts of information at our fingertips and exponentially increased our ability to produce more, faster, yet it's sped up our lives and tattered our capacity for deep contemplation.

For a few moments we took turns poking our heads around the boulder at the top of Qua Qua to look at the rest of the island below us and at the whitecaps on the sea, dainty little creases in a blue tablecloth. But every time we stepped from the shelter of the boulder the wind hit us straight on, chilling our sweat. I was too tired and too preoccupied with thinking about the hike back to feel any emotional connection with Columbus's damn trade winds, plus we could see a storm moving toward us, and if the trail got any muddier it would make the downhill ordeal even worse. The view was pretty nice, but not worth hanging around for. We'd made it to the top, and that was enough. Now we had things to do, comforts to get back to.

That evening, back in the room, I told Lynn, "I found myself thinking during the hike that if I had a heart attack up there, what my last message would be for Mike and Dave to carry back to you."

"What was it?" she asked.

Temporarily safe, I laughed. "None of your business," I told her.

Everybody has to believe in something. Even nihilists' nothing gives some shape to their worldview. Lynn, a non-observing Catholic, now genuflected before psychoanalysis. Psychoanalysis helped her develop a deep quality and appreciation of her life and although she didn't proselytize for it, she believed in it fervently and insisted it can help many people whose lives fall short of where they would like it to be...that psychoanalysis can make life better for anyone who'd be willing to embrace its fundamental tenets. Just to tease her certainty I sometimes insisted that writing can do much of the job of therapy.

Meanwhile, during our week in Grenada I'd run the air conditioner in my room and driven around the island burning gas and spewing emissions. None of this was enough to make any difference in climate change, so why not? I believe that I have a moral obligation to our species and to everything else on the planet, but it's not as if there's anything I can do that really matters, is there? So I recycled whenever I could, and when I left my hotel room I turned the air conditioner on low. Outside our room, as twilight faded to dark and the birds sang themselves to sleep, I stared into the night sky and wondered, does *anything* matter?

iv

We hope that our existence will echo beyond our corporeal end. It raises some basic questions: what *are* we doing here and does it matter whether anyone else cares, from our lover lying beside us in bed to whatever immanence, intentional and sentient toward us or not, lies beyond the sky? In these days of climate change, writing, raising kids, doing good work, leaving our marks may all ultimately be useless pastimes but some of the most important pastimes we have. Graffiti taggers, lovers who carve their initials into a tree, our ancestors who painted on their cave walls, believe in two things: that their art has some kind of effect and that the universe at least hears us when we declare, "I am." Does it make any sense then to worry about climate change?

Those moments in which we transcend or sweeten our awareness of time give us respite from the knowledge that someday whatever we've left behind of possessions, writing, and memories, whatever impact we've made, will eventually fade and then disappear out of memory, like a faded photograph of us that will one day get ruined by a careless splash of coffee or end up in the hands of a stranger who bought it at a curio shop. Even the ashes in the urn will one day find their original place in the universe. Once in a small Nebraska town I stumbled across an estate sale. The estate sale guy had placed everything the dead old lady had owned on long tables that circled her huge front yard: furniture, silverware, tablecloths, curtains, a pencil from Frank's Hardware, scratch paper pads, post cards and letters, a road map so old that Interstate 80 appeared only as a ghostly planned projection (had she gone on a trip long ago, and if so, with whom?), embroidered napkins, candles, clothes, bottles of perfume, tubes of ointments and salves, a flyswatter, ruler and yardstick, needles, pins, buttons and threads, playing cards, photographs of people….For many things, it was impossible to tell which had been the fabric of her life and which were only detritus. When everything had been sold, the crowd, led by the auctioneer, filed inside the house and bid on the air conditioners, the radiators, the furnace, and the hot water heater, and then the house itself went up for auction until everything about her had been dispersed. I still have her roadmap and keep meaning to put it in plastic, but it's so yellowed and fragile that I'm afraid to touch it.

The evening after our Qua Qua hike we went to dinner at a friend's house high on a hill above the lights of Grenada. Looking at the stars, Vishnu, a Hindi, told us, "We believe that the universe began as just one thing, an incredibly tight compressed ball." A subatomic piñata. The primal seed. All that has burst from this compressed ball is still part of it, still expanding, just as a flower opens and its pollen and seeds create other flowers, just as a sperm chimes against an egg, snuggles its head inside, and both are consumed in and transformed by their embrace. Behold the cauliflower or broccoli, how each smaller piece looks like a miniature of the head it came from. Bend down to eye level with the moss in the tundra, look closely, and you will see a forest. Just as bacteria and virus and amoeba unfurled into fish, amphibians, reptiles, and mammals, we are all part of the continual developing cosmos, neither in the center nor on the edges, our history and future only this: everything, including us, is stardust; all things are both forged inside of and part of the furnace of creation. Hope is a candle in the desert night, a skyrocket that bursts, disperses, and absorbs into the sky, but while it lasts it has its value, pleasures, and thrills.

Chapter Thirty-One:
Cherry Blossoms

Until the late twentieth century, every generation lived with the tacit certainty that there would be generations to follow.....Hardships, failures and personal death were encompassed in that vaster assurance of continuity. That certainty is now lost to us, whatever our politics. That loss, measured and immeasurable, is the pivotal psychological reality of our time.—Joanna Macy, "Working Through Environmental Despair"

Giving it up

Is there really any difference between facing our individual end and living through the denouement of our species? Fortunately, I'm a little better prepared to think about these things than most: I've pondered mortality most of my life. When I was a child, every time I saw a shooting star I felt a brief thrill, followed by sadness and a slight fear: I believed they were dying stars, and I'd think someday there wouldn't be any stars left. I used to delight in shouting into canyons, seeing how long my echo would reverberate, my disappointment growing as it faded. Whenever I skipped a stone across the water, the minute it left my hand I hoped against hope it would skip forever. Later, I held my breath whenever a space shuttle returned, hoping it wouldn't hit the atmosphere at the wrong angle and bounce off into space, or come in too sharply and disappear in a bloom of incineration.

In elementary school, we had occasional air raid drills. When the warning bells rang, the teacher turned off the classroom lights, and we dutifully crouched under our desks, putting our coats over our heads. It was a welcome relief from the boredom of school. Occasionally while we crouched during the drills, I'd hear a plane overhead, and I'd think: is this really it? Would our coats really protect us from an atom bomb? Could I make it home through the fire and chaos? None of these fears rose to the level of panic. Hiding under the desk, I'd think it would be safer in the teacher's closet than under the desk, and if I could make it there without getting caught, I'd even have a chance to see what was in her coat pockets and purse. The thought came not from larceny but hope, and hope is tied in to curiosity.

When I was about seven years old I began to suspect that although I'd come close, I would probably not be around when we finally landed a man on Mars. (In 1953, I never imagined that it might be a woman). Once I raced an airplane on my tricycle. Even though I knew it flew hundreds of miles an hour, I saw it moving slowly across the sky, and I figured that with enough effort I could outrace time and distance. (I might have won too if I hadn't come to a busy street). My family tree is riddled with cancer, and in my twenties I realized that there'd probably be no cure for cancer during my lifetime. "To discover a cure for cancer, we'll have to discover the secret of life," Doc Rosenblum once told my father, a view reflecting not so much science as old Doc Rosenblum's scientific and philosophical limitations.

Throughout my life, hope and fear have jostled against each other. Even back in the days of nuclear anxiety, I felt that annihilation wasn't *really* imminent. We could probably survive a nuclear attack. And it might not even happen: the second before pressing the red button, even the worst human being might still hesitate, if only out of fear of mutually assured destruction. In these days of accelerating climate change though, the train has left the station. When fear marries with scientific certainty, when hard science tells you that your train is hurtling toward the gorge where the bridge and trestle are already blown, you can try running until you reach the end of the last car, but then what?

Climate change is the ultimate terror, the end of everything. More minor terrors have acquired the imprimatur of The Name We Dare Not Speak, and so we can whisper their names, shiver and thrill to them in melodramas, murder mysteries, and horror movies. If the setting is secure enough—around a campfire, at pajama parties, in Fundamentalist churches—we still scare our children and ourselves with tales, but the implicit message is that we've all got a chance of being saved if we stick together or if God backs us up. With climate change, however, the largest destructive force we have ever faced, the fuse seems lit and we can't seem to yank it out. Do we have any defense other than denial?

We still flinch, turn away from genuinely accepting our ultimate reality. Several years ago I stopped bringing up climate change around potential or new parents and in discussions with my financial person about my retirement portfolio. All these people believe in their plans and future, and it's not my place to upend their apple cart. I wouldn't have wanted to stop Johnny Appleseed by telling him that someday DDT, Alar and Roundup would seep into the groundwater and the eggshells of eagles. He was a good man with good intentions, more power to him. He may not have saved the world but he made it a better place.

When I was nearing seventy years old, I began to realize that even though I'd prefer a seat at the grand finale, I'd probably miss the climactic *sturm unt drang* at the end of the Anthropogenic Era. *Quelle dommage*, meaning both "too bad" and "what extraordinary damage is coming down the pike." When squirrels gather food in late autumn, does it feel different to them than it does in summer: does the leisurely summer foraging become a frantic urge to store up for the oncoming winter? Does anxiety exist on a purely biological level or does it require some knowledge of the future? One recent morning I heard a robin chirping, and I realized that it was mid-summer and I'd seen fewer robins that year. As I watched it hop around looking for worms, I anthropomorphized: poor, brave, lonely thing. Since then, more flora and fauna have disappeared. Butterflies, bees, and frogs have dwindled, though goddamned mosquitoes seem to have gained ground. Just like so many parties I've been at, the first to leave are the ones you hoped would stick around, and the last to leave are the ones you're irritated at.

I console myself by thinking about the upside of climate change. All those cheesy self-help books will finally reveal their true nature: decorative nests on the side of a crumbling cliff. And I'll be hearing a lot of Barber's *Adagio for Strings* and the Adagietto from *Mahler's Fifth*, that exquisitely melancholic music. Keats, walking in the woods, heard a nightingale's beautiful song and was surprised to discover he felt sad; beauty exists, he realized, *because* it's ephemeral. *Sic semper homo sapiens.*

What matters at the road's end?

In his prophetic novel *The Road,* Cormac McCarthy posed the penultimate question: in the final days of our species is there any reason for living, any meaning to our existing? He created the perfect laboratory for examining the questions: nothing on Earth will ever grow again, which means that what little food remains is finite, and a father and his young son walk through the world of ashes trying to survive. Along the way they dodge gangs who kill and eat others. The father has a gun with just a few bullets. He intends, when the predators are closing in, to shoot his son and himself. But why keep going? Why not do it now?

Primitive paintings on dim cave walls, the aspiration and great fall of the Tower of Babel, the statues of Easter Island, the Aztec and Incan temples, the pyramids all speak about people's hopes about their place in the universe. I once imagined myself in a spacesuit cut loose from my tether, slowly tumbling off into the vast black cosmos, the remainder of my life measured by the dropping oxygen gauge, spending my last minutes inside my hermetically sealed bubble singing aloud and laughing at my fantasy that I'd finally made it to Carnegie Hall. Maybe I could even laugh at the vainglorious Great Pharaohs who ordered their names and their lives' high points inscribed on the tombs that were built for them while they were still alive; they couldn't imagine that invaders and looters would dare to break into their tombs after their deaths, scratching out their names and stealing their possessions. Later Pharaohs tried new wrinkles in the arms race, etching their names deeper into stone, and then eschewing pyramids and hiding their tombs in secret caves. Meanwhile invaders were removing the gleaming white limestone that covered the Great Pyramid of Khufu and carting off the stones to build their own mosques and forts—the ultimate fuck you and abnegation of the Pharaoh: it isn't *you* who will live forever in people's memory, it's *Us*. We're all Pharaohs and Queens in our own lives, and I'm still my father's boy: my anxious father Herb used to compensate for his own thwarted dreams by sitting on his bathroom throne working a crossword puzzle. Geoglyphs scratched centuries ago into the desert floors of Arizona by the Anasazi are now surrounded by fences to protect them from Visigoths who have found meaning in their lives by driving over them in their ATVs.

In the dusk of the Anthropogenic Era, will we finally realize that our braggadocio, greed and preening, our quarrels, feuds, and wars, didn't justify the toll of misery and lives, and will we allow all of those to precipitate away until only our sense of grace and love remains? Or will we fall back on the fang and claw, determined to eke out every last moment of survival? Because of the perspective our consciousness affords us, we have a unique challenge: figuring out how to live through our final days. And when our species disappears, will it matter whether our final resonance was a fierce, futile fight for survival or whether our final resonance was our capacity to create and appreciate beauty, love, music, writing, and art?

Our desire to survive is fueled by the combustion of hope and denial. I liberally season it with humor as well, merrily whistling past the graveyard.

You laugh or you cry

Thank you all for coming out to see me tonight in this awful weather. Mark Twain said that everybody talks about the weather but no one does anything about it. Boy, he should have been living today. Any climate change deniers in the crowd tonight? You know, close to eighty percent of Americans believe in angels, which is why some of you will ride your horse off a cliff waiting for the horse to change into a unicorn.

I'm right there with you: sure, some people are getting worried about climate change, but I think the way technology's developing we'll figure out a way to digitize the environment. Those people who keep complaining about what's happening to the environment, why don't they just go live somewhere else if they don't like it? Besides, Nature's already re-finding her balance; there's fewer fireflies around to heat things up. I'm telling you, this is the best of times to be living in. Yesterday some guy wanted to pick a fight with me for cutting in front of him and I said, "Do you really think this is worth fighting about with the end of the Anthropogenic era coming?" Remember how Novembers used to suck in Chicago? Today this guy comes up to me on the street and says, "Isn't this great weather for November?" I said, "Well, it presages the end of civilization as we know it, but at least it's not 35 degrees and sleeting." Don't get me wrong, it's not like there are no downsides to climate change. Already the scam artists are making money off it. I sent in $175 for a How to Survive Climate Change Kit, and they sent me a copy of Kafka's *Metamorphosis*.

But look, now's not the time to give up hope: I figure Nature's almost at the point where she'll realize she needs us and she'll be forced to negotiate. And all that ice in the Arctic, who needs it? It wasn't doing anything except clogging up the Earth's sinuses. By the way, you know the difference between the Gulf Coast and Bangladesh? The Gulf Coast doesn't flood as often yet. Say, what about those rising sea levels? Pretty soon America's holiday will be the Firth of July. But, hey, none of this stuff matters anyway; civilization's only a social construct.

How about some entertainment news? They're predicting climate change will be next summer's blockbuster. And the latest issue of *Conde Nast's Traveler* magazine showcases the 10 Best Resorts to Witness the End of Civilization From. By the way, I see that God just announced He's planning to close His long-running production of The Anthropogenic Era. "It's been quite a run," He said, "but now even the theater's getting pretty run down." Asked about His future plans, God revealed only that He plans to focus His creative energies elsewhere.

But seriously folks....

Memories and possessions

When Alex returned to Chicago after she graduated college, she quickly found a job and her own apartment. For nine years after that, her bedroom in the apartment had remained pretty much the same—stuff in her drawers, posters on the wall, a futon, blankets which I washed once in a while to get rid of the dust, and an old dresser that one afternoon she and her middle-school friends decorated with indelible magic markers. Her books, accumulated since grammar school, were on a bookshelf in another room, alongside a cork bulletin board with a few photographs and a notice from the State of Illinois that as a newly licensed driver her license was now on probation because of a well-earned speeding ticket in Wisconsin. (Well-earned not because she was going nineteen over the limit but because a few hours before she drove off I told her, "Make sure you don't speed in Wisconsin. They're really tough on out of state speeders.")

Finally she came over to go through her things and decide what to donate, what to toss, and what to take with her. Crawling under her bed, we found a few dusty duffle bags that we opened with trepidation. Whatever was in there smelled so musty that we quickly zipped up the bags without inventorying the contents, ran them outside, and tossed them in the dumpster. She ended up leaving almost everything else in my apartment. The problem is, she revealed, she was thinking about moving across the country to either Austin or Portland, so it didn't really make sense to bring more things to her own apartment right now. The news, and her taking away only about half of her stuff, didn't seem to hit me too hard. Lynn and I had worked out an arrangement where I stayed at her condo four nights a week, so now I only semi-lived in Alex's and my place.

Besides, I told myself, I didn't believe in hanging on to the past any more fervently than I believed in looking forward to the future, and that Alex's lingering presence in the house said something only about my inertia. But that evening I felt ambushed by sorrow, and it hung on me for weeks. In my seventy years, I'd undergone two major prunings of possessions I once thought so valuable that I joked after my death I'd either have them buried with me like a pharaoh, or that my lover, relatives and friends would go through them and spend hours reminiscing about me and reassessing who I really was.

The prunings consisted mostly of old T-shirts, over-wrought writing, report cards, birthday cards, letters, my high school yearbook, redundant photographs, a lot of film negatives, and some certificates for achievements that didn't seem too meaningful even when I got them. The first great extinction was during the 1960's—an era marked by an upheaval of values. So much of my generation was excited, defiant, adrift and moving around the country that I remember asking someone where she considered her home. "My junk drawer's in a dresser in my parent's house in Boston," she said. The second extinction came a quarter century later when I moved into Sandy's home, caused by a combination of not enough room for much of my stuff nor, on both our parts, much perceived need for it. I did keep some classroom photos from grade school, and it surprised me that I remembered the first and last name of every single person in the photos. One of the girls in my 4th grade classroom photo had scratch marks over her face; a friend and I had decided we didn't like her and tapped her face a few times (in the photo) with a tack hammer. The year before I'd googled my friend, who I hadn't seen or heard of in over fifty years and found his obituary:

he'd become a big entertainment lawyer in LA and the year before he'd choked to death in a restaurant on a piece of food.

Alex and I both ended up making different excuses for leaving much of her stuff behind and maintaining her presence in the apartment, but our excuses covered up a deeper reason that was redolent with some mourning for the passing of the past and some anxiety about the future. How do you know when an era really ends anyway?

Enjoy yourself,
It's later than you think,
Enjoy yourself,
While you're still in the pink

Whatever the Earth eventually evolves into, we will not be around to see it, not even the 1% who are already building environmentally enclosed fortresses which will prove to be little more than the tombstones of social Darwinists who embrace the denial of the fittest. The Etch-a-Sketch will eventually be wiped clean of us; a Finger has already begun to twist the knob, erase the slate. The lunatics who walk the sidewalks with their signs proclaiming the end is nigh are becoming like the hypochondriac's famous last words on his deathbed: "I *told* you I was sick."

The main road is the one we try to avoid with denial; it's as though we keep reading about travel without putting down our smart phones or leaving our easy chairs. We don't give ourselves a chance to discover that fear and sorrow are seldom as unbearable as our defenses and anxiety warn us they are. Ideally, as we approach closer to death, our dance of hope and denial slows; the two lifelong partners embrace more tightly until they merge into something that approximates peace and may even become peace itself. Ultimately the most important thing is how we will go through our end times, which is at least partly a matter of choice. We may go out in an avalanche of misery, a manic or ecstatic joyride, a beautiful sorrow, a handbasket to hell, or we may just drift off into a cloud. Me, rather than protecting my food and water with a semi-automatic, I hope to leave feeling peaceful, content.

A few years ago I was sitting on a too-crowded beach in Michigan, morosely swatting sand fleas while Lynn napped without a care in the world. I mapped out the rest of the day, vacation's end. We'd have to leave in an hour and a half, wash off as much of the damned sand as we could so we wouldn't get too much of it in the car, find somewhere to change clothes, and start our hour and a half drive to Chicago, hoping to get there ahead of the end-of-weekend traffic, which meant we wouldn't have time to stop and eat anywhere, and I was already hungry. Then we'd have to unload the car. I *told* her she'd brought too much damn stuff.

I killed time watching a middle-aged guy build a small sandcastle while his kids cavorted in the water. People sauntered, strode and slogged past without noticing him and his work. I watched him spray parts of his castle with a water bottle and, using a small pointed stick to make little designs on the walls, he dug out windows and molded turrets. The sands of Egypt, the sands of Michigan. He carefully, slowly poured little pebbles just a few at a time from a pail, making a tiny road to the castle and escalloping the walls. I wondered at what point a compulsive act becomes peaceful, the artist merges with his art? I eyed the waves lapping onto the beach and was irrationally relieved to note that his castle would be safe for several hours. I considered going over and talking to him, but he was so intent I didn't want to disturb him.

When the castle-builder and his family left, I walked over to take a closer look. I thought about digging a trench around the castle to extend its existence. A good thirty years ago, walking in a park on one of those mild, end of summer days, I saw someone way off sitting cross-legged, so still and erect that I knew he was meditating. I walked closer and saw him smiling with his eyes closed. Not having believed in vibes since my days of acid trips, I nevertheless felt his aura. Looking at the sand castle thirty years later, I remembered him and felt his peacefulness again. The smallest acts can reverberate, endure, change how we and others experience the world.

A.E. Housman always resonated with me, something my poet friends tolerate just because they like me. Housman rhymes; the few times he does associative leaps, you can follow them, and you always know what his poems are telling you: outdated stuff, all that. "Loveliest of Trees, the Cherry Now" has only twelve lines. During Easter season, Housman looks at a blossoming cherry tree, and he does the rueful math from Psalm 90:10: a man is allotted seventy years—threescore years and ten—and twenty of those have already passed for him. Cherry blossoms, a sign of spring, last only a short time, their white spring bloom resembling snow. Christianity and most other religions have sugarcoated death by promising an afterlife, but Housman will have none of it:

> And since to look at things in bloom
> 50 springs is little room,
> About the woodlands I will go
> To see the cherry hung with snow.

I've been in Washington, DC when the cherry blossoms appear, but I didn't really understand their resonance until I went to Japan, where cherry blossoms are both a reminder that the world has beauty, and that the beauty is over before you know it. The moment doesn't need us; we need the moment. Better to take the time to appreciate the mortality, beauty, and irony of things. The delicate and ephemeral cherry blossoms appear during the gateway of spring, blooming pure and already ghostly. In a panorama that covers nearly half a wall inside Tokyo's National Museum of Modern Art, *Parting Spring*, Kawai Gyokudo's two six-fold screens begins with a cherry tree at the head of a gorge above a peaceful river, shedding its blossoms into a gentle breeze; the blossoms waft down the gorge, downriver, until finally they become wind-driven snowflakes blowing over a rough, gray sea. Buddhist monks work for months carefully creating intricate sand mandalas and mark the completion by destroying them. Cherry blossoms, calligraphy, meditation, sand mandalas remind us to slow down and appreciate time, appreciate life. We haven't been nearly good enough at savoring and conserving the things on our planet that could have sustained us. We still have time to do some of that. If we can give up the delusion that salvation leads to something beyond our life span, we can still find the salvation that's left for us.

PART SIX:
THE LAST DROP

SISYPHUS AND HIS FATE

*I*n his essay "The Myth of Sisyphus," Camus pondered the plight of Sisyphus, who was condemned to roll a heavy boulder up a mountain. Every time Sisyphus neared the top, the boulder rolled all the way back down to the bottom. This was his fate, his life for eternity, and he knew it. Camus wondered whether it was possible for Sisyphus to find any joy or meaning in his existence and concluded that it was. Don't look too far ahead or behind. Feel the glorious exertion of muscle and sweat. Each immediate moment that you can exult in defeats time and the punishing gods.

Chapter Thirty-two:
Delayed Reactions

A few months after I'd returned from the Pecos, my poet friend Barry Silesky told me, "You'll be retelling this story for the rest of your life." I thought he was cautioning me not to become a bore who'd tell my story so many times that I'd wring all the drama and life from it until relating it would become a mere dutiful or compulsive act, tiring even to me. But he meant something wiser: rather than calcify into something fixed and dull, the experience would continue to resonate and evolve. I once heard someone ask a psychoanalyst, "How can I tell when my analysis is over?" The analyst replied that discovery is an ongoing process. That doesn't mean we should stay in analysis forever, he said. But however discovery happens, whether we do it willingly or unwillingly, aware or unaware, assisted or unassisted, our search matters.

How each of us continues on our journey—with friends, lovers, family, with a professional guide—is our decision, though it seems to me that our guideposts should be personal relationships rather than money or power.

Of course there are explanations for how and why we've gotten to where we are at—decisions we're made (or didn't make) basic biology, and various values and emotional imperatives passed down from one generation to another. But mysteries and questions keep evolving about how and why I got lost in the Pecos and came to the brink of death. Mysteries and questions about why I did what I did to get to that moment on the fulcrum, and why I did what I did immediately afterward, and with the rest of my life.

Here is *what* I know. Given my backpacking experience, I made surprising mistakes in the Pecos. Although I can explain the reasoning that led to each mistake, the accumulation of them suggests something more than coincidence and random bad breaks. Did I really want to die? To test myself to find out whether I actually wanted to live by playing for even higher stakes than when I hitchhiked or dropped acid in the sensory deprivation tank and tried to go out of my body?

What I *do* know is this: after I'd found my way down to the trickle of river, hoping I was getting close to the safety of a campground, I saw cold campfire remains and horse hoof tracks in the mud, and I plunged ahead following the river until I ended up lost so far in the wild that the rescue team and I had to trek for several hours until we could get to a place where horses could finally reach us and then another half hour getting me to a place where a helicopter could land. A few days after I'd been rescued, I traced my journey on a topo map and discovered that only about 20 yards from the horse tracks and campfire remains, visible if I'd just looked, there was a dirt path that led less than a hundred yards to a paved road. Instead I plunged deep into the wilderness.

For several years after the Pecos, I believed that I'd decided to live because of Alex, that my hallucinations of her face seared the realization of love and responsibility into my brain. This gave coherence and purpose to my life, kept me going in the Pecos and in the years after the divorce. Then one day I realized that I have a large framed photograph of three year old me looking just a little off center from the camera, and the expression on my face is the same expression I'd hallucinated on Alex's face: sorrow, fear, and a tremulous hope.

Chapter Thirty-three:
The Path to the Cave

In a recurring dream, I'm hiking toward a cave, and while I'm dreaming I realize that I remember this path and this cave from other times and that I've never actually made it all the way up. The path feels familiar but also new, and afterward in the early fog of awakening the hike has felt so real that I wonder at first whether the cave in my dreams is actually a cave I've been to in my waking life, one that has slipped below the edge of my conscious memory. But as I awaken more and lay in bed with the growing knowledge that I have not reached the destination once again, and as the details, minutia, responsibilities, diversions, excitements, and thoughts of everyday life sweep away the familiarity of the dream hike, I slowly realize that I've never really seen this place. In fact, the cave could not exist, because its path begins on a rocky path in a warm desert, and within minutes of not-so-steep climbing, I enter fields of ice and snow, though the air stays pleasantly warm. Although the trail begins close to a campground that's heavily used, the trailhead is isolated and semi-hidden, so no one other than me ever seems to be know about it or walk on it. In one dream I took some friends with me, but they didn't want to continue, and I decided not to go on alone: that dream was mildly disappointing; sometimes we pay a price for friendship. Once my father, whom I've seldom dreamed about since his death, has been in the campground, though he stayed behind and didn't walk along the path with me.

I never make it to the cave. I just know that I'm walking the path as an amalgamation of ant and human being, the ant impelled to do what it does and go where it's headed driven by biological imperative, and the human walking with curiosity and apprehension. In my many other dreams of this theme in which I can't finish something or don't get where I need to go— trying to catch a plane, leave a house, get packed, tell someone something important, save myself from the devil, murderers, or police—I wake anxious, knowing that a dream has just gotten my day off to a lousy start and hoping that a shower will wash it away. But in my path to the cave dream I feel a vague excitement when I wake, bemused but not regretful that I haven't reached my destination. Instead of disappointment, I feel a kind of wonder that once again I've walked this mysterious path that I know so little and so well, and I start my day pleased to find that even after over 70 years of dreaming, I can still spend time in a world that's both known and unknown, familiar and a mystery, a world in which there's still something to explore. After all, beyond new restaurants and questions such as what's eternity and what's beyond the universe, what really remains to find out about?

I've refused to attempt an autopsy or analysis of my cave dream, to freeze and dissect it. I choose to hold this dream differently from my others. I'm afraid that analyzing it will ensure that I never dream it again or, worse, will leave me with nothing to look forward to in my final moments. I've decided to let the mystery just simmer and breathe.

I think that maybe the purpose and meaning of this dream lies in my future, not my past. I hope that as I slip into death, I'll be walking that path again. Along the path everyone I've known, including people I've forgotten, will nod or wave as I pass, until finally I leave them all behind, knowing that this time I'm actually going to make it to the cave. As someone back in the room says, "He's gone," I'll reach its entrance, having discarded everything except for what I've decided has remained most important to me, whatever that will be. At that moment, I might pause and leave even those things outside. Or I might carry them inside. I'll find out when I finally make it there.

EPILOGUE:
Advance Notice

October, 1989

Dear Alex,

The weather here is autumn crisp, the clouds are moving faster across the sky, and the leaves, depending upon my mood, are either going out in their final blaze of glory, or shrieking in red and gasping in yellow. You'll be arriving a few weeks after the winter solstice, when our world's thirsting for extra light. You'll find things are a bit problematic here, so try to hold on to whatever you're bringing with you. I wish I could prepare you for what you're coming into, but there are limits to what even I can do. A few months ago your mother and I went to a Cubs game, and someone right behind us kept whistling so shrilly that I worried it was piercing inside her and jangling your nerves. Reasonably, I knew I couldn't tell him to tone it down; I could only hope he'd pass out from the beers and sun. The Cubs took over first place that game—something that will happen only a few times during your life—and there was this joyous, roaring energy in Wrigley Field I hadn't felt anything similar to since Mardi Gras.

Inside your mother, can you tell the difference between the adrenaline of joy and the adrenaline of terror?

While she's been carrying you, your mother and I have walked among the pyramids and temples of Egypt, and I toyed with the idea that you were absorbing some primitive vibrations. You're closer than I am to knowing whether the Egyptians were right about those boat rides to and from the afterlife.

Although I know that none of these experiences of your mother and me will matter much to you, shortly after you develop a sense about yourself your memories will begin to accumulate. Memories are more than just mental snapshots; they coat the heart and brain. Almost everything you will experience will pass through the smoke of memory.

Part of your essential history is that you were conceived in New Orleans during Jazz Fest. You mother and I were in love, and music drifted down the streets all day and night. Although there will be many times when love and music seem far away and even occasionally out of reach, for now you're in the most protective cocoon of your life—so protected that we're thinking of you before you are thinking of you. During your life, often unknown to you, others will love you and think of you at random moments, and the irrational hope is that if enough people do this you'll be more protected from harm.

After you're born, our imagining who you are will undoubtedly affect your life—not as much as we might like, more than you will someday prefer, and in ways none of us can predict. Imagination has genuine power. For a while you'll believe absolutely in its power, and then you may spend too much of your life forgetting about it. Always tend to your imagination: it has such an awesome fragility.

But these days you don't have to worry about any of this; you can just relax and enjoy the connection between you and your mother with roots that stretch back into mists. Here you are curled right in the center of Mother, where the umbilical cord connects to placenta which washes in the blood that runs swiftly down the riverways of her body through her heart and across her brain, and I sometimes imagine the two of you whisper to each other in dreams.

This is as good time as any, I suppose, to tell you that the difference between a star in the throes of creation and the moment of your conception is a difference only in size. If we had ears large enough to hear the one and small enough to hear the other, they would sound the same. The *moment of your conception is an echo of the creation of the universe.*

Well, today's street cleaning day, and I have to go move the car to the other side of the street before it gets ticketed. The world can get pretty complicated. There's probably more to say about that, but I'll catch you later.

Dad

Acknowledgments

So many people have helped in various ways to bring *Last Drop* into the world. My Chicago writer friends Sharon Solwitz, S.L. Wisenberg, Barry Silesky, and Chris Grimes are masters of feedback who also sprinkle in just enough hosannahs. Lucy Freund and Bonnie Spring helped keep me believing that I really could, and should, get my memoir published. Gail Cooper Markunas read an earlier draft and not only fact checked but kept it honest. Obviously, *Last Drop* couldn't have been created without all the good friends and lovers in my life who, by being who they were, anchored, sparked and taught me what relationships and life can be; my gratefulness for that is the kind of gratefulness that can never be repaid enough. And special thanks to Spuyten Duyvil, the spitting devil angels of Brooklyn who keep alive the idea that good writing matters and that publishing has a mission deeper than the bottom line.

GARRY COOPER is a writer and psychotherapist in Chicago and Oak Park, IL. A Professor at Prescott College, he teaches Masters candidates in Counseling, where he emphasizes doing effective therapy by understanding each person instead of over-focusing on the "problem." It's a good recipe for living in general. As a finalist in Nottinghill Editions' 2015 International Essay contest and Midwest Review's 2019 Great Midwest Writing Contest, he finally decided to go for the whole enchilada and publish his own memoir with Spuyten Duyvil. A former Contributing Editor of *Psychotherapy Networker*, his essays and articles have appeared in *Tusculum Review, Fatal Flaw, Blue Mountain Review, Another Chicago Magazine, Triquarterly, Rockhurst Review, Bloodroot, Psychotherapy Networker,* and *Perigee.*

www.ingramcontent.com/pod-product-compliance
Lightning Source LLC
Chambersburg PA
CBHW011233120626
46549CB00009B/3257